Equal opportunities and recruitment

Equal opportunities and recruitment

How Census data can help employers to assess their practices

Shirley Dex and Kingsley Purdam

JOSEPH ROWNTREE
FOUNDATION

The **Joseph Rowntree Foundation** has supported this project as part of its programme of research and innovative development projects, which it hopes will be of value to policy makers, practitioners and service users. The facts presented and views expressed in this report are, however, those of the authors and not necessarily those of the Foundation.

Joseph Rowntree Foundation
The Homestead, 40 Water End, York YO30 6WP
Website: www.jrf.org.uk

About the authors
Shirley Dex is a Professor at the Institute of Education, University of London

Kingsley Purdam is a Researcher at the Centre for Census and Survey Research, University of Manchester

ISBN 1 85935 399 1   (paperback)
ISBN 1 85935 400 9   (pdf: available at www.jrf.org.uk)

A CIP catalogue record for this report is available from the British Library.

Cover design by Adkins Design

Prepared and printed by:
York Publishing Services Ltd
64 Hallfield Road
Layerthorpe
York YO31 7ZQ
Tel: 01904 430033;   Fax: 01904 430868;   Website: www.yps-publishing.co.uk

Further copies of this report, or any other JRF publication, can be obtained either from the JRF website (www.jrf.org.uk/bookshop/) or from our distributor, York Publishing Services Ltd, at the above address.

Contents

Data that would allow employers to examine robustly whether their practices might be discriminatory has been unavailable in the UK. However, the 2001 Census data, with its extended range of questions over earlier Censuses, appeared to offer a new opportunity for employers to be provided with data about the available pool of qualified workers from which they could draw. Employers could assess their own workforce recruitment statistics in comparison with those in the available pool. As in the USA, such data can shed light on employment and selection practices (Coussey and Jackson, 1991).

This project set out to explore the extent to which the 2001 UK Census data could be useful to employers in evaluating their recruitment practices. The project has involved a number of phases. First, we investigated more closely how the USA system works. Second, we recruited a number of UK employers to provide case study data about their own policies, practices, data collection and monitoring. Third, these employers were also asked to participate further in using the Census data and statistics, alongside their own organisation statistics. This third phase aimed to provide 2001 Census data about relevant pools of qualified applicants for the jobs that these employers regularly advertise and who they recruit to help in the monitoring process.

The main areas of discrimination we set out to consider were race and gender. We recognised that minority ethnic groups vary considerably in their labour market status, as well as in other respects. This means ideally that one should examine separately the prevalence of each minority ethnic group in any specific geographical area.

We were also interested to examine disability and age discrimination. But again we were aware from the outset that there would be more problems with obtaining data with sufficient sample sizes to offer reliable statistics. Nonetheless, our report does consider these other types of equal opportunities monitoring and the data required.

Why monitor?

Monitoring workforce profiles and applicant profiles can give an insight into the effectiveness of the equal opportunities and recruitment practices, both in relation to the organisation as a whole and in relation to specific job types (Brown and Gay, 1985). The Commission for Racial Equality (CRE) has campaigned for ethnic monitoring since the early 1980s, as have other organisations such as the Institute of Personnel Management. The CRE produced a new ethnic monitoring guide for local authorities in 2002, which argued that, without monitoring, an organisation will never know whether its commitments to equal opportunities are working (CRE, 2002a).

There are many examples of how monitoring has led to an improvement in opportunities and diversity in the workforce (Hepple *et al.*, 2000; CRE, 2001b, 2003a). As Stevenson *et al.* (1988) argued, monitoring gives equal opportunities credibility and integrity. It would be possible to counterpose monitoring with engaging in other activities, for example, positive action or outreach. However, without monitoring, it is not clear whether other such activities are having any effect. Moreover, as monitoring of the workforce is a basic foundation for evaluating the extent of diversity, it is also one of the central ways to investigate whether organisations' internal procedures and practices are being non-discriminatory.

Monitoring has long been part of codes of practice attached to discrimination legislation from its inception and subsequently (CRE, 2001b, 2003a). Since 2001, there has been a requirement for public sector organisations to monitor the ethnic composition of their workforce. However, the extent to which these practices will be introduced across the private sector is unclear.

For organisations to take their equal opportunities (EO) policies seriously requires them to carry out a number of procedures, as described in Coussey and Jackson (1991), namely to:

1   collect data on their workforce which contains information about the categories covered by the EO policy

2   monitor this data regularly to see if minority groups are doing as well as majority groups

3   assess whether further investigation is needed to ensure equal opportunities is a reality and follow it up with appropriate action

4   examine and monitor the processes of recruitment, selection and promotion to make sure they are not either directly or indirectly discriminatory

5   provide training in EO procedures for staff involved in decision making.

In principle, the within-organisation elements of these procedures are not inherently problematic. Once individuals are working within an organisation, it is not difficult to keep records of all employees, their grade, length of service, qualifications and their personal characteristics as covered by EO policies (ethnic origin, gender, disability, marital status). The extent to which UK employers carried out some of these procedures for a range of categories of discrimination was reviewed in Hepple *et al.* (2000) and is shown in Figure 1. The summary findings suggested that many British employers in 1998 were not taking seriously the implementation of their equal opportunities policies. Many organisations in Britain did not keep records; of those who kept records, few analysed them.

Current situation

Following the new requirements on race discrimination in 2001, a major survey of public authorities by the Commission for Racial Equality (CRE, 2003c) found that only just over one-third of organisations were responding well to both the spirit and the letter of the new duties. Though the vast majority of public organisations had produced a race equality scheme or policy.

The private sector, not subject to the 2001 legislation, had different experiences. A survey of 500 UK directors in 2003 found that, while almost three-quarters stated that their businesses had a policy in place to promote equal opportunities, far fewer had the systems in place to analyse workplace diversity (Joseph, 2003).

Figure 1 Extent of equal opportunities policies and monitoring in a nationally representative sample of GB workplaces, 1998

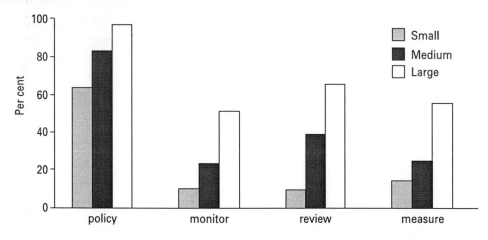

Source: Workplace Employee Relations Survey (WERS), 1998. Figure published in Hepple, B. Coussey, M. and Choudhury, T. (2002) *Equality: A New Framework, Report of the Independent Review of the Enforcement of UK Anti discrimination Legislation.* University of Cambridge, Centre for Public Law and the Judge Institute of Management (2000, p. 17).

Notes: Policy: employers with formal equal opportunities policy
Monitor: monitor promotions be gender, ethnicity
Review: review procedures for indirect discrimination
Measure: effects of EOP

Only 38 per cent of directors stated that their organisation collected information on the number of employees by ethnic group. Only 22 per cent stated that their organisations collected information on job title or grade and ethnic group, and only 31 per cent collected information on job title or grade by gender (Joseph, 2003).[1] Research by the law firm DLA, which surveyed human resource professionals across 1,400 employers in the public and private sector, revealed that only 38 per cent of employers monitored the diversity of their workforce and that 71 per cent of employers stated that they did not benchmark their activities in the areas of diversity and equality against key comparators. Approximately one-half of employers stated that equality and diversity issues did not feature in their organisation's performance system (DLA, 2003). The research also found that human resource professionals felt there was a lack of support for diversity issues among senior management and 40 per cent felt that diversity and equality issues were not integrated throughout their organisation or were part of its culture (DLA, 2003). Hoque and Noon (1999) found that companies' statements about equal opportunities in general and equal opportunities statements in particular were not necessarily indicators of good practice.

Further research by Hoque and Noon (2001), examining the responses of almost 24,000 employees in 1,880 different workplaces, found that only a minority of employers (12 per cent) had what could be termed strong equal opportunities policies, i.e. policies that were meaningfully enforced through positive action measures and monitoring procedures.[2]

The studies reviewed above also suggested that many employers were far from prepared for the introduction of new anti-discrimination legislation relating to religion and sexual orientation in December 2003. Moreover, in relation to age discrimination in the workplace, research by the Employers Forum on Age (EFA, 1999) and more recent research by the DfEE (2001) found only limited awareness of the Government's Code of Practice on Age Diversity and very few employers were implementing changes in line with the Code of Practice.

There are more issues to face if organisations are to consider the possibility of discrimination in the recruitment and selection of employees, assuming all vacancies are advertised. Questions that need to be addressed include the following:

- do qualified employees of all groups apply for advertised posts in proportion to their presence in the population?

- given the population of qualified applicants who do apply, does each group have the same chance of getting on the shortlist?

- given the applicants that get on the shortlist, does each group have the same chance of getting offered the job?

Data external to the organisation is required to answer the first question. The proportions of majority and minority (or gender) applicants need to be compared with the proportions of appropriately qualified populations of majority and minority groups who are potential applicants for the vacancy in question. Where the distributions of applicants, offers or hiring outcomes by majority/minority group deviate, in a statistically significant sense, from their distribution in the relevant qualified populations, then discrimination may be present and this possibility needs further investigation.

On this area of monitoring, little could be done prior to 2000 because of the relatively poor data resources available in the UK. The 1991 Census data contained information about the labour market position of ethnic minorities (Bhavnani, 1994; Owen, 1994a; also in a series of Census statistical papers at Warwick University, see Owen, 1994b). Many regions drew out statistics on minority ethnic group proportions in the total or regional population, across all age groups. But this includes children, people beyond working age and those who are not seeking work. The distributions across different socio-economic categories were also available at a national level for a number of minority groups. However, this data was not sufficiently detailed to enable employers to have an accurate test for discrimination of their own practices or to allow employers to identify likely pools of suitably qualified applicants in the relevant spatial labour market.

The availability of a new data source in the 2001 Census made it worth considering whether it was possible to improve on these earlier statistics, to help employers carry out more effective monitoring.

Is monitoring really necessary?

We could well ask whether monitoring is really necessary. To answer this question we need to consider further whether discrimination still exists in the UK, and also whether it might wither away on its own without a legal framework.

UK research that has tried to measure the extent of discrimination over time has shown that discrimination against ethnic minorities continues to exist despite legislation (reviewed for ethnic minorities up to the early 1990s in Dex, 1992; Esmail and Everington, 1993, 1997; and for MBAs in Hoque and Noon, 1999), albeit at lower levels than in the past. The investigation of race discrimination has been subjected to situation testing, which involves sending matched applicants to apply for advertised vacancies and monitors what happens to them. Research using this kind of methodology has also been conducted in relation to people with disabilities. For all types of discrimination where legislation has already been passed, there are ongoing cases in employment tribunals of discrimination (see Liff, 1999; CRE, 2003b; EOC, 2000) and differential experiences in the labour market continue to persist.

There are other studies that offer evidence of race and gender discrimination (Modood and Berthoud, 1997; Berthoud, 2000; Cabinet Office, 2003). Research by the Department for Work and Pensions (DWP, 2003a) highlights that the labour market circumstances of ethnic minorities vary regionally and that, even after taking into account qualifications, age, gender and disabilities and whether people were born in the UK or not, there are still substantial differences in the likelihood of ethnic minorities being in employment compared to the white population. Research has shown that ethnic minorities are substantially under-represented in local government employment (which includes the fire service, police, schools and colleges controlled by the local authority) and hugely under-represented in the senior civil service (DWP, 2003b). Heath and Cheung (2004) have also highlighted the persistent earnings gap between Caribbean, Pakistani and Bangladeshi men and the white population, with these minority populations earning between 20 and 40 per cent less.

Wide-ranging discrimination in the labour market has been found in relation to people with disabilities (Burchardt, 2000, 2004; Smith and Twomey, 2002; Goodlad and Riddell, 2005). In 2002, there were 1.1 million disabled people in Great Britain seeking work. Analysis of the Labour Force Survey (LFS) suggests people with disabilities are only half as likely to be employed as those without disabilities (Goodlad and Riddell, 2005). Unemployment rates among people with disabilities were 7 per cent in 2004 compared to 4 per cent for non-disabled people. Around half of people with disabilities are estimated to be economically inactive compared to the national rate of around 15 per cent. Moreover, LFS data suggests that disabled people who have had a job have longer periods out of work than non-disabled people. Evidence suggests many disabled people want to work (DRC, 2004). Burchardt (2004) found that disabled people accounted for half of all the working-age population in 2003 who were not in work but wanted a job. In research by Graham *et al.* (1990), identical job applications were submitted but one application declared that the applicant had a non-work-limiting disability. Again it was found that the disability severely affected the likelihood of the candidate being invited for interview. For further discussion of the implementation of the DDA through the employment tribunal system see Hurstfield *et al.* (2004).

Research by the Performance and Innovation Unit (PIU) has suggested that discrimination on the grounds of age is substantial (PIU, 2000; DWP, 2002). Of respondents in research conducted by the Department for Education and Employment, 20 per cent stated that they had experienced age discrimination (DfEE, 2001). The research available in relation to discrimination in employment on the basis of religion or sexual orientation is very limited.

When effective monitoring and follow-up action are implemented it does appear to produce a more diverse workforce (Hepple *et al.*, 2000; CRE, 2002a). Research by the Cabinet Office (2003) found that, across the civil service, the employment of minority ethnic staff has increased substantially to 9.7 per cent on average but the presence of ethnic minorities is concentrated in the lower scales. In senior grades, ethnic minorities make up on average only 2.8 per cent of the workforce and there are some departments with no ethnic minorities in senior posts. There is also considerable variation across different departments. One of the shortcomings of early targets and monitoring – for example, in relation to disability – is that the targets did not consider job type or grade or geographic variations in the number of people with a disability (Coombes, 1997).

The fact that discrimination persists despite the legislation suggests that it is not easily going to wither away without society as a whole making more effort to get rid of it.

Plan of this report

The various phases of this project are described in the rest of this report. In Chapter 2, we summarise the case study employers we recruited to be part of this study. In Chapter 3, we describe the datasets in more detail, their availability, advantages and disadvantages for this task. Some comparisons are also drawn here with USA data available to employers for monitoring. In Chapter 4, we present some illustrations of how statistical data can be used as part of employers' monitoring processes. Finally, in Chapter 5, we have a more general discussion about monitoring equal opportunities in the UK and present our conclusions.

2 Employer case studies

Introduction

The first stage of the research focused on gathering information on the types of workforce data and databases collected and maintained by a number of case study employers. We felt we needed a good understanding of a range of employers' recruitment practices, job specifications and workforce characteristics in order to see how far available data could help them in their monitoring processes.

It was recognised that, ultimately, the outputs from this project would aim to reach all employers, both small and large, advanced and backward, in implementing and monitoring equal opportunities. However, to illustrate the full extent of what could be done with population data sources, we needed to recruit employers who were reasonably well advanced in their commitment to equal opportunities, and in data collection and collation of relevant applicants' and workforce data. This meant recruiting both reasonably large employers who were committed to equal opportunities and public sector employers who were all obliged to act on statutory requirements. The organisations were selected through liaison with contacts provided by the Advisory Group for this project, local knowledge, employers identified in relevant newsletters and a presentation by the research team to a group of potentially appropriate employers. It was surprising to find that, even among these purposively selected case study employers, there were serious limitations in the scope and accuracy of employers' data and in job definitions.

Interviews were initially conducted with nine employers' representatives over the autumn of 2001 into 2002. One further employer was recruited later in the project. In total, five public sector organisations, four private sector organisations and one voluntary sector organisation were recruited. The employers' representatives interviewed were either human resources directors or personnel officers who were responsible for equal opportunities, or specialist equal opportunities directors. All organisations were enthusiastic about the research and keen to participate further.

In addition, discussions were held and help for the project was given by representatives of the Commission for Racial Equality and the Equal Opportunities Commission. Trade union representatives in each organisation were also informed about the research.

Content of interviews

The content of the semi-structured interviews covered a range of topics under a number of main headings as follows:

- nature of business and types of jobs covered

- profile of workforce – numbers in different jobs (ask in advance) (by ethnicity, gender, age and disability)

- recruitment process, criteria used and spatial areas for recruitment

- databases/records kept about applicants and staff by type of staff and grade/level

- equal opportunities policies, practices and monitoring

- barriers employers saw to using the Census data and to collecting data from applicants.

Further detail on the topics is provided in Appendix 1.

Key findings

All the case study organisations had a written equal opportunities policy. These varied slightly in the employee characteristics they covered, although all included characteristics of gender, ethnicity and disability, there being a legal requirement to comply at the time the interview took place. Some employers were thinking ahead to new legislative requirements and others had a long-standing recognition that a diverse workforce involved having employees with a very wide range of characteristics.

Data collection on applicants

All employers stated that they collected data on gender, ethnicity, age and address. Several organisations also collected data on disability and working time. The data collected and stored about individual employee or applicants' characteristics was not always as extensive as the characteristics listed in their equal opportunities policy documents. It was felt to be too sensitive to ask people regularly to disclose some of their characteristics, for example their sexual orientation or religion.

All the organisations used an equal opportunities monitoring form, which applicants for vacancies were asked to fill in as a voluntary exercise. The characteristics covered by each employer's equal opportunities form for applicants are displayed in Table 1. There were varying degrees of success in the proportions of applicants filling in these forms. There was also substantial variation in the questions and categories covered on the form, particularly with respect to the question asking applicants to self-define their ethnicity. Some organisations were using 1991 Census categories for ethnicity while others had developed their own set. Other organisations, having devised a set of their own categories, were in the process of changing them to be in line with the 2001 Census groupings. On the whole, public sector organisations were well ahead of private sector organisations in collecting data for equal opportunities monitoring. However, hardly any of these organisations were analysing their data.

> ### Box 3 Employer 1: private, manufacturing (100,000+ employees in several sites across the UK)
>
> This employer had one central database of all employee records. The database includes information on home address, age, gender, ethnicity and disability. However, the information on ethnicity and disability was very incomplete. As a result, this employer found producing profile statistics difficult and had to rely on management classification for missing data via specific company-wide audits. The actual database was managed by a sister company and any requests for breakdowns had to be added to the existing contract. This was a barrier to regular analysis.
>
> Graduate recruitment, which made up a substantial part of new staff each year, was the most automated. Applications were initially made online and information on an applicant's ethnicity was collected. The employer had done some initial analysis of applications by ethnicity and was acting on the results.

Table 1 Summary of case study employers' applicant data collection and contents of workforce database (Part 1)

Case study employer and sector	Workforce database — Variables collected[a]										
	Age	Gender	Ethnicity	Disability	Religion	Working time	Marital status	Grade/Job	Geography	Caring responsibility	Data quality or completion problems
1 Private, manufacturing (Eng)	✓	✓	✓	✓					✓		✓
2 Private, retail (MYO)	✓	✓	✓	✓	✓			✓	✓		✓
3 Private, retail (ClotheYou)	✓	✓	✓			✓		✓	✓		
4 Private, retail\manufacturing (Energise)	✓	✓	✓	✓					✓		✓
5 Public, local authority (NorthLA)	✓	✓	✓	✓				✓	✓		✓
6 Public, service (Transit)	✓	✓	✓						✓		✓
7 Public, service (ED-NW)	✓	✓	✓	✓			✓	✓	✓		✓
8 Public, service (PublicServ)	✓	✓	✓	✓				✓	✓		✓
9 Voluntary sector, service (YouthWork)	✓	✓	✓	✓			✓		✓	✓	
10 Public, service (ED-SE)	*	*	*	*	*	*	*	*	*	*	✓

*   Information was not collected from this employer, although the employer does collect data on some of these variables.

a   For some employers, different variables would be used at different stages of the recruitment process.

Table 1 Summary of case study employers' applicant data collection and contents of workforce database (Part 2)

Case study employer and sector	Applicant data Variables collected[a]								Collate and analyse applicant data (G = graduate)
	Age	Gender	Ethnicity	Disability	Nationality	Marital status	Geography	Qualification	
1 Private, manufacturing (Eng)	✓	✓	✓		✓	✓	✓	✓	G only
2 Private, retail (MYO)	✓	✓	✓	✓			✓	✓	✓
3 Private, retail (ClotheYou)	✓	✓	✓	✓			✓	✓	
4 Private, retail\manufacturing (Energise)	✓	✓	✓		✓		✓	✓	G only
5 Public, local authority (NorthLA)	✓	✓	✓	✓			✓	✓	
6 Public, service (Transit)	✓	✓	✓	✓	✓		✓	✓	✓
7 Public, service (ED-NW)	✓	✓	✓	✓		✓	✓	✓	
8 Public, service (PublicServ)	✓	✓	✓	✓		✓	✓	✓	✓
9 Voluntary sector, service (YouthWork)	✓	✓	✓	✓		✓	✓	✓	✓
10 Public, service (ED-SE)	✓	✓	✓	✓			✓		✓

* *Information not collected.*

a *For some employers, different variables would be used at different stages of the recruitment process.*

Box 4 Employer 2: private, retail (32,000+ employees in sites throughout the UK)

This employer had a central recruitment point for the majority of posts. This was linked to a central database of employees, applicants and potential candidates. The initial application form included a section on equal opportunities monitoring and asked for details on age, ethnicity (1991 Census categories) and gender. There was a problem with the completion of these forms and with particular issues such as disability.

For store work, the emphasis was on skills, experience and enthusiasm rather than on qualifications. The employer used a lot of in-store advertising. If there was a vacancy in a store or a new store was opening, its manager was sent a selection of applicants' details but only their work experience and hobbies but not details on gender, ethnicity or disability. The manager would then select a shortlist and only then was sent the full details of candidates including their name, age, address and ethnicity. The shortlisted candidates were interviewed. The manager then had to feed back why he/she had selected certain candidates and not others. If a candidate withdrew, they also had to follow this up.

All new employees were asked to complete a second form. This requested information on age, gender, ethnic origin, disability and religion (Northern Ireland). However, the completion rate for this form had fallen from 85 to 55 per cent in recent years. Despite this missing data, the employer was able to produce a breakdown of the workforce. The database was updated regularly. The employer also produced area Census data for new store managers so that they could attempt to reflect the local population in their workforce.

Box 5 Employer 4: private, retail/manufacturing (exact number of global employees unsure but very large)

This is an international organisation. The employer had conducted a number of initiatives around ethnicity and gender, and had set targets for 2008. It was keen to reflect the local population but the issue of global diversity and international recruitment complicated the issue. The employer was unsure how to resolve this. The employer had a worldwide HR function and system database, which included information on age, ethnicity, disability and medical information. It was not in a position to provide a detailed workforce breakdown by job type.

(Continued)

The employer had a large-scale graduate recruitment programme. This was online. There was an optional diversity and equal employment monitoring form. The questions varied according to the country of recruitment and local laws and what was felt to be appropriate. For administrative posts, the organisation tended to use agencies and then take on selected staff more permanently.

Box 6 Employer 5: public, local authority (23,000+ employees in one local area)

At the time of the interview, this employer was also conducting an update survey of staff details, including collecting information on disability. It was unhappy with the quality of the information it had got as the information was self-specified. It also wanted to update the ethnicity categories to those used in the 2001 Census. This was the first update for three years and the employer was hoping for a response rate of 60 per cent. In the past, there had been a problem with how seriously the forms had been taken by staff and a reluctance to give particular information. The employer has introduced a 'not stated' category on the new form.

It did not collate or analyse information on applicants. It kept only hard copies, though, in the past, it had done some pilot studies of applicants' profiles. The employer also compiled a range of workforce data in relation to Best Value.

Box 7 Employer 7: public, service (7,000 employees in one local area)

For this employer the central database of employee information was attached to payroll but there were a number of gaps in this data. The employer estimated that 60 to 65 per cent of equal opportunities forms were not returned. Often applicants did not download the form. Others did not return it and there was no system for chasing this up but changes were being planned. Of present staff, the employer estimated that 15 per cent of records were incomplete. The manager said 'there seems to be a reluctance to give the information'.

The employer has conducted some initial analysis comparing its workforce to the local population on an ad hoc basis but this was limited because of problems with its records – at the time. There was no systematic analysis of the data. It was able to produce some statistics in relation to headline figures and job sector but not by scale. It was also unsure about how it categorised the ethnicity of employees from overseas.

> **Box 8 Employer 8: public, service (13,000 employees across one region)**
>
> This employer had conducted a range of recruitment campaigns and aimed for national targets set by the Government.
>
> The employer had a comprehensive database of information on employees. It was able to produce employee profiles for the day of our actual meeting by area, gender, ethnicity and grade. All application forms included an equal opportunities monitoring form and, if these were not returned with the application form, they were chased up, as it is very much part of the application process. Ethnicity and disability workforce data was seen as important. All applicants from black and minority ethnic communities or those with a disability were offered a general interview.

Outsourcing the recruitment process to another organisation posed problems to the equal opportunities data collection and monitoring. The same problems applied where the employer was part of a very large multinational organisation and where some recruitment was done centrally, even in a different country or by internal movements between the subsidiary units or country sites of the organisation.

Applicant data collation and analysis

The collation, use and accessibility of the data from applicants' forms varied considerably across different employers. Though the information was collected, some organisations did not have systems in place to enter it into a database or, even when it was entered, to analyse it. There was also considerable variation in the detail and scope of databases kept and in relation to particular variables. One organisation produced detailed applicant and employee statistics on gender, ethnicity and job grade to the day of the interview and could produce information on demand. Other organisations were able to produce only limited headline statistics using management classifications for some categories or in relation to ethnic group having coded the missing individuals as 'other'. Often the data was one year or more old. Though in some cases, it was linked to financial reporting periods.

Several employers just kept copies of applicants' forms and made no further examination or use of the data collected. All organisations admitted that there were many gaps in their data, partly as a result of a lack of importance given to the equal opportunities monitoring forms both by staff and by the organisation as a whole.

Several organisations had initiated a resurvey of staff but these surveys had low response rates. Other organisations were planning such surveys. All the employers interviewed stated that they were in various stages of upgrading their employee databases.

Employee databases

There were similar variations in the quality and range of data kept in databases about existing employees (see Table 1 earlier in this chapter for the detail of the characteristics covered). Employers commented that it was difficult to keep these up to date. The attempts to fill in gaps, described above, were not wholly successful, so there was much missing data on important equality characteristics. It appeared that relatively little use was made of the databases in either equal opportunities monitoring, or more general workforce planning or strategy. In part this was because the quality of the data was not sufficiently reliable or complete. Public sector organisations were in the process of trying to upgrade their databases in order to deal with their new legal duties. But, when our interviews were carried out, half of the public sector employers included here were far from having adequate databases or systems for data analysis.

In one organisation, the workforce database was managed by a sister company. Being one step removed from access to the database was a significant barrier to using this data in any meaningful way on a regular basis.

Criteria used in recruitment and selection

In all organisations, every vacancy had a person-specification form. Many of these specifications emphasised personal skills such as observation and self-regulation rather than actual qualifications for certain types of work. For more senior posts, there was often a requirement of minimum or specific professional qualifications.

This specification went along with an advertisement placed in appropriate media and on the organisation's website in some cases. The level of advertisement, not surprisingly, related to the grade of post. Advertising was done locally and, where high-level specific qualifications were required, specialists press outlets were used along with posting vacancies on websites.

This aspect of the review of organisations' recruitment procedures was instructive. The job criteria drawn up ranged along a spectrum from wholly specific to very general and, as such, had varying degrees of being possible to match to data that are regularly collected in surveys or by the Census. Some of the jobs advertised were so specialised that it would be impossible to ever hope to gain information from nationally representative surveys or even Census data about the pool of qualified applicants. Box 9 gives examples where specific requirements would be impossible to match to an occupational coding category used in any of the large-scale official datasets. These sorts of criteria posed natural limits to employers' abilities to use Census or other data to help in their monitoring equal opportunities.

Box 9 Examples of specialist criteria mentioned in job specifications

- Specialist knowledge and skills in safety, quality and environment (SQE) techniques, and a good understanding of the SQE legislation and standards is essential.

- Experience of developing, implementing and monitoring prosecution and investigation exercises to detect fraud, evasion, irregularities and other forms of revenue loss or bylaw offences.

- Five years of experience.

- Experience of fund raising.

- Knowledge of new government initiatives and policies.

- Full knowledge of Quark, Photoshop, Illustrator, Dreamweaver or Homesite and proficient in HTML.

- Highly experienced in SAP configuration and implementation. Proven track record in managing SAP projects.

Other organisations had devised their own tests to give to applicants at an early stage of the process in order to filter out people who could not meet a necessary minimum standard of physical competence for the job. These competencies involved physical fitness in one case, good eyesight and quick reaction speeds in others. These were felt by employers to be necessary to cover their responsibilities for public safety. Such characteristics are again not currently regular parts of large-scale surveys or Census data collection. However, it is reasonable to assume that they are distributed equally across all ethnic groups and between men and women.[1] They are likely to vary by age, in which case the appropriate group to use as a comparison standard in monitoring would be the relevant age group drawn from the overall working population in the relevant recruitment area.

However, there was a range of jobs where it was likely to be possible to match data to the job criteria sufficiently to provide helpful pointers about the likely pool of qualified applicants for such jobs. A match to data containing information about individuals' highest qualifications would be possible for some graduate entry programmes that have a degree requirement not restricted to one particular subject area. Also the recruitment of qualified engineers is a similar possibility, where the dataset contains information on occupations and possibly highest qualifications. In addition, a range of jobs with lower-level qualification requirements could be matched to the Census data where the criteria specified could be translated into the NVQ level and where this educational level was contained in the dataset. However, it is often not the lowest levels of jobs (or qualification levels) that equal opportunities policies are aimed at measuring, but instead how individuals progress to the top levels of jobs. Where employers are monitoring progression, the appropriate match would be success rates of each ethnic group or women or men.

How do people apply?

The majority of the employers required paper entry forms for applications. At the time of interview, only two of the organisations offered a web-based application process and this was only for their graduate recruitment programme where large numbers were expected to apply.

Spatial areas of recruitment

Organisations were broadly aware of the spatial areas from which their employees were recruited. Generally, the lower the grade (and pay) of the job, the more local the address of the employee and vice versa for higher-grade jobs. There was an awareness that commuting distances were on the increase in some jobs. Organisations' advertising strategies for vacancies reflected this awareness with local outlets for lower-grade or starter entry jobs and national outlets for higher-grade entry jobs. At the same time there was recognition in several organisations that it was important to reflect their local population. However, no attempt was made by any of these organisations to analyse the postcode or addresses data of their employees to see exactly where they travelled to work from.

Most employers were aware of the profile of the population in their local areas. One organisation provided each of its stores with a Census breakdown of the local population by ethnicity, though it was left to managers' discretion whether any use was made of this.

Equal opportunities initiatives

Despite the general lack of analysis of workforce data, employers were aware of the imbalances in their workforce and many had drawn up initiatives to try and reach out to recruit a more diverse population. Examples of these initiatives are included in Box 10. Two of these organisations had set five-year targets for recruitment of minority ethnic and gender groups.

Box 10 Examples of initiatives to broaden the diversity of employers' workforces

■ Long-term gender and ethnicity workforce targets.

■ Recruitment events, roadshows and presentations targeted at minority ethnic groups.

■ Recruitment campaigns targeted at older people.

■ Gender and minority ethnic group promotion initiatives.

■ Introductory days for target groups.

■ Links with schools – school visits.

■ Bring your daughter to work days.

Comparisons with company regulation in the USA

The contrast of these UK case study organisations with USA companies could not be more striking. There are, of course, legal requirements in the USA for affirmative action. This requires all public organisations and organisations wishing to contract with government to draw up an affirmative action plan (AAP) and update it annually. Since the vast majority of large USA companies do contract with government in some way, the coverage of this law is widespread.

The procedures that USA employers are expected to carry out are described in Employment Policy Foundation (1991). Companies need to submit annually to the Bureau of Labor an affirmative action report (EEO-1 report) on their workforce broken down by white/non-white categories (see Figure 2). They also face legal requirements to keep records and collect data (see Box 11). Figures from this report are fed into a computer along with details of their local area's workforce from the Census.

Figure 2 Part of the USA Government's annual EEO-1 report form for the private sector

SF 100 Page 2

Section D—EMPLOYMENT DATA

Employment at this establishment—Report all permanent full-time and part-time employees including apprentices and on-the-job trainees unless specifically excluded as set forth in the instructions. Enter the appropriate figures on all lines and in all columns. Blank spaces will be considered as zeros.

JOB CATEGORIES		OVERALL TOTALS (SUM OF COL. B THRU K)	MALE					FEMALE				
			WHITE (NOT OF HISPANIC ORIGIN)	BLACK (NOT OF HISPANIC ORIGIN)	HISPANIC	ASIAN OR PACIFIC ISLANDER	AMERICAN INDIAN OR ALASKAN NATIVE	WHITE (NOT OF HISPANIC ORIGIN)	BLACK (NOT OF HISPANIC ORIGIN)	HISPANIC	ASIAN OR PACIFIC ISLANDER	AMERICAN INDIAN OR ALASKAN NATIVE
		A	B	C	D	E	F	G	H	I	J	K
Officials and Managers	1											
Professionals	2											
Technicians	3											
Sales Workers	4											
Office and Clerical	5											
Craft Workers (Skilled)	6											
Operatives (Semi-Skilled)	7											
Laborers (Unskilled)	8											
Service Workers	9											
TOTAL	10											
Total employment reported in previous EEO-1 report	11											

NOTE: Omit questions 1 and 2 on the Consolidated Report.

1. Date(s) of payroll period used: 2. Does this establishment employ apprentices? 1 ☐ Yes 2 ☐ No

Section E—ESTABLISHMENT INFORMATION (Omit on the Consolidated Report)

1. What is the major activity of this establishment? (Be specific, i.e., manufacturing steel castings, retail grocer, wholesale plumbing supplies, title insurance, etc. Include the specific type of product or type of service provided, as well as the principal business or industrial activity.)

OFFICE USE ONLY

g.

Section F—REMARKS

Use this item to give any identification data appearing on last report which differs from that given above, explain major changes in composition of reporting units and other pertinent information.

Section G—CERTIFICATION (See Instructions G)

Check one

1 ☐ All reports are accurate and were prepared in accordance with the instructions (check on consolidated only)
2 ☐ This report is accurate and was prepared in accordance with the instructions.

Name of Certifying Official	Title	Signature	Date
Name of person to contact regarding this report (Type or print)	Address (Number and Street)		
Title	City and State	ZIP Code	Telephone Number (Including Area Code)	Extension

All reports and information obtained from individual reports will be kept confidential as required by Section 709(e) of Title VII. WILLFULLY FALSE STATEMENTS ON THIS REPORT ARE PUNISHABLE BY LAW, U.S. CODE, TITLE 18, SECTION 1001.

Box 11 USA record-keeping requirements for employers

Title VII of Civil Rights Act 1964 for employers of 15 or more employees

Annual EEO-1 report (applications and other personnel records – promotions, transfers, demotions, lay-offs, terminations – temporary and seasonal positions.

Executive order 11246 for government contractors and subcontractors with 50 or more employees and a contract of $50,000 or more (in 2000)

Records considered to be support for the affirmative action plans.

Rehabilitation Act 1973 for government contractors and subcontractors with 50 or more employees and a contract of $2,500 or more (in 2000)

Affirmative action plan for the handicapped.

Age discrimination in Employment Act (ADEA) 1967, 1978, 1986 – for employers of 20 or more employees

- Payroll or other records, including those for temporary positions, showing employees' names, addresses, dates of birth, occupations, rates of pay and weekly compensation.

- Applications (personnel records relating to promotions, demotions, transfers, selection for training, lay-off, recall, discharge, job orders, test papers, employment physicals, job advertisements and postings, copies of employee benefit plans, seniority systems and merit systems).

Equal Pay Act – all employers engaged in interstate commerce

Payroll records including time cards, wage rates, additions to and deductions from wages paid, records explaining gender-based wage differentials.

Americans with Disabilities Act 1990 – employers of 15 or more employees

Applications and other personnel records (promotions, transfers, demotions, lay-offs, terminations) and requests for reasonable accommodation.

Uniform Guidelines on employee selection procedures – employers subject to Title VII or Exec. Order 11246 with 100 or more employees

Records showing impact of the selection process for each job by gender and ethnic/racial group that constitutes at least 2 per cent of the labour force in the relevant labour area or 2 per cent of the applicable workforce, including, but not limited to, applications tests and other selection procedures used as a basis for employment decisions, hiring, promotion, demotion, training and termination.

The computer runs a check across companies recruiting in the same local area, given its local working population, as to whether they are managing to produce an ethnically and gender diverse workforce. If one company is not managing to do this, but another one in the same local area is, the former company is thrown up for an investigation and has a 10 per cent chance each year of being investigated. Where investigated companies can show they have records and paperwork to justify all of their recruitment and promotion decisions, and have made recruitment efforts to address the workforce imbalances, the Government is happy to leave it at that. Where this is not the case, a more in-depth and longer investigation takes place, which has been known to last years in some cases. Companies live in fear and dread of being investigated. They feel is it very bad for public relations and their reputation.

In 2001, in the USA, only companies with 50 or more employees and more than $50,000 per annum turnover were required to submit annual EEO-1 reports. This was under review with a view to increasing the threshold to $100,000 per annum turnover.

Against this background, the majority of large USA organisations and companies put considerable effort into complying with the law's requirements on equal opportunities. The companies visited in the course of this project were undoubtedly among the most serious about complying with the law, seeing it as a positive opportunity to make sure they had a diverse workforce, representative of their local populations. What was striking was the level of resources they devoted to the monitoring exercise in terms of staffing and specialist databases and software requirements. Each of the large companies had directors of equal opportunities on every site. In addition, at least two or three full-time employees worked on maintaining the workforce EO database, carrying out annual analyses and preparing the annual EEO-1 report. Annual analyses of the travel-to-work areas of employees were also carried out, examining whether any changes in the transport system and infrastructure had occurred that would affect the spatial area from which potential recruitment could take place. There were also employees in the recruitment sections of the companies whose job was dedicated to seeking out minority-group recruits and opportunities to contact minority groups. In addition, there was a high level of data collection and maintenance on workforce characteristics (much of it required by law), a high level of written files and stored justifications of all recruitment and promotion decisions, and criteria on individual applicants as well as on the stock of employees. One of the USA organisations contacted was worried about its website recruitment process, especially for graduates, and was in the process of discussing this with the US Bureau of Labor. This employer was faced with thousands of website enquiries and informal approaches, the majority of which did not turn into serious applicants for jobs.

Where USA companies outsourced their recruitment, they were legally required to make sure the same data was collected and equal opportunities procedures followed as if they were doing it themselves.

The USA companies stood out from comparable UK equivalents in the levels of data collected, its level of completeness, the maintenance of databases, analyses of the data collected, familiarity with the analysis issues, the person-power resources set aside to work on this and the written justifications for all decisions. Companies' representatives who were interviewed, although all wanting to argue that equal opportunities and a diverse workforce were very good for business, were also aware that the legal framework in the USA was responsible for the level of resources that USA companies put into implementing and monitoring equal opportunities. Hepple *et al.* (2000, p. 123) also noted that USA employers spoke of a turning point arriving with the legislation on contract compliance requirements.[2]

This USA comparison has salutary lessons for equal opportunities in the UK. Where many UK employers, thought to be at the best-practice end of implementing equal opportunities, do not even collect or collate adequate data about their workforces, it is difficult to see how monitoring will ever be genuinely effective in the UK. Of course, part of the problem is that the relevant information is available from individuals only on a voluntary basis. In the USA, since employers are given no option but to collect data on every individual applicant and employee, individuals are given little choice but to agree to provide the information if they wish to be employed at all.

Conclusions

The time we spent with the organisations in the UK and USA was very useful in showing us about their recruitment practices, their selection criteria and where the provision of external data may be able to help. Our investigation was also helpful in showing us where external data is unlikely to be able to assist in equal opportunities monitoring. The poor state of UK organisations' databases became apparent, especially in comparison with those in the USA. This was particularly striking in view of the UK organisations having been selected on the basis of being thought to be using best-practice procedures. We managed to achieve only a small number of case studies with up-to-date and reasonably complete data about the workforce and data about applicants broken down by gender, disability or minority ethnic identity. This low number of examples is sufficient for offering illustrations for this report, but does not offer an optimistic picture of the amount of monitoring that can be carried out within UK organisations.

What was also striking about the USA organisations was the level of human resources they devoted to data collection, monitoring and analysing their data. This was substantially larger than any resource inputs committed to these functions in the UK organisations. Obviously, the legal requirements take away any choice in this matter for USA organisations, as compared to UK organisations.

The comparison with the USA led us to question how far private UK companies will go in implementing and monitoring equal opportunities policies on the largely voluntary basis they are currently allowed to operate. Changes in data collection are clearly the necessary starting point for more effective monitoring in the UK. Although data collection requirements have increased for the public sector, there is still the problem about incompleteness and quality of the data that need to be addressed.

3 Available data

Introduction

In this chapter, we examine the datasets available in the UK and their potential to assist employers in monitoring equal opportunities in their workforce. We consider two datasets only – the 2001 UK Census and the Labour Force Survey. These are the only datasets likely to offer samples of sufficient size for analyses of minority ethnic groups as well as containing other necessary information. (See Boxes 12 and 13 for a brief description of the two datasets.)

Box 12 2001 UK Census data

The UK Census data for 2001 is the most comprehensive data on the population resident in the UK. It is certainly the largest data source on minority ethnic populations in the UK. Moreover, categories for collecting data about minority ethnic identity are devised for the Census and tend to influence categories used in all other official datasets. The 2001 Census obtained responses from 94 per cent of the population. Non-response was estimated to be higher for young men and those living in urban areas.

Box 13 The quarterly Labour Force Survey

The quarterly Labour Force Survey is a rolling household-based sample survey of individuals across the UK focusing on participation in the labour market. Individuals stay in the survey for five successive quarters and are dropped on a rotating basis. The LFS collects core information on: industry sectors, type of work and occupation; earnings; qualification levels; economic activity; alongside other personal characteristics (age, gender, disability status, ethnic identity). In particular years, additional questions are included. In each quarter, interviews are achieved at approximately 59,000 addresses with 138,000 individuals. Although it is a very large survey, individuals from particular minority ethnic groups are low in number in any one year's sample. Larger groupings sufficient to carry out some analyses are possible by pooling several years of data. Analyses at levels of geography below region also run into problems of small sample sizes. There is also an annual LFS (LLFS) consisting of quarterly LFS

(Continued)

data (waves 1 and 5 interviews) and boost data. The boost data covers local and unitary authorities across England, Scotland and Wales in order to obtain more reliable estimates at these geographical levels. This LLFS data has most but not all of the variables of interest to this study.[1]

The 2001 Census collects all the required information: geographical detail, educational qualifications, detailed occupational information and ethnic group. However, we have not been able to obtain this information in a single table or datafile. The options are briefly reviewed.

- *Published tables* for the Census are freely available but, while the geographical detail is available, any given table contains insufficient detail on other variables.

- *Commissioned tables* : the Office for National Statistics (ONS) allows users to specify tables that meet their own requirements. Although this has the potential to meet a number of our data requirements, the delay in obtaining commissioned tables (over 11 months) closed off this option for this project.

- *Samples of Anonymised Records* drawn from the Census: our original plans were to use these samples of microdata from the 2001 Census. These files were expected to contain sufficient detail to meet all the project requirements. However, unexpected changes to disclosure rules at ONS have meant that the geographical detail required is not available and, in many cases, there is inadequate occupational information.

- *Controlled access microdata samples* (CAMS), which provide the level of detail needed for the study, became available towards the end of the project, but only by going to ONS at Titchfield and working in a safe setting. The tables shown later in this report use data from the CAMS. However, the restrictions on access mean that this is not a viable option to use beyond a pilot study.

Demographic characteristics required

For the purposes of this project, a number of individuals' characteristics were potentially relevant. Gender, ethnic identity and disability are all of central and current interest because of the existing anti-discrimination legislation based on these characteristics. In addition, because of forthcoming legislation, data on individuals' ages and religion will be important in the near future.

The other characteristics that are important to carrying out any monitoring with these data are as follows.

■ *Age* – necessary to identify those in the population who are of working age, e.g. 17 to 65 inclusive, and excluding those who are either too young or too old to join the pool of qualified applicants.

■ *Economic activity status* – necessary if we wish to exclude from the available pool of working population those who are unable to work, or possibly do not want to work.

■ *Occupation or socio-economic status* – necessary if we wish to analyse recruitment for particular qualified jobs, e.g. teachers or engineers.

■ *Highest educational qualifications* – necessary if we wish to analyse the general educational level required for particular jobs.

■ *Geography indicator* – this identifier is necessary if we are to examine the available pool of applicants in any defined local area. To be as useful as possible, the level of geographical identifier for each individual in the data needs to be for as small an area as possible. This is to offer the opportunity to add these small area units together in a flexible way in order to match, as closely as possible, an area around the employer's address, which will be their likely recruitment area.

The two datasets under consideration contain identifiers for most of these characteristics (see Table 2). However, the level of detail provided by each and scale of geography vary considerably. In addition, the sample sizes for local areas and minority ethnic groups vary in a way that sets limits to the analyses that are possible.

It is notable that 16 categories covering ethnic identity in the 2001 Census are starting to be disputed in practitioner publications (see JNCHES, 2004).

Access to the data sources

When this project was conceived, we did not envisage any access problems to the Census or LFS data, but both access and the nature of the available Samples of Anonymised Records Census microdata changed over the life of this project, as described below.

Table 2 Details of datasets

Individual characteristics	England and Wales 2001 Census	Quarterly Labour Force Sample Survey
Gender	√	√
Ethnic identity	√ (Based on new 16-category definition devised for Census)**	√ (Based on new 16-category definition devised for Census since 2001. Only available for certain local areas)
Disability*	X (General health or only those with long-term limiting illness)	√ (DDA disability status and health past and present)
Age	√	√ (16+)
Religion	√	√
Economic activity	√	√
Occupation/SOC*	√	√
Highest education qualification	√ (Based on NVQ)	√ (More detailed educational and qualification categories but can be recoded to NVQ system)
Geography level*	√ (Region, local authority district and lower for limited tabular output)	√ (Region and local authority district)

* See Appendix 2 for more detail on these categories.
  DDA = Disability Discrimination Act.
** In Scotland, there were 14 categories for ethnicity and fewer in Northern Ireland.

The quarterly Labour Force micro datasets continue to be available free for academic use (with charges for other funded research or commercial uses). These datasets are not particularly easy for employers to access and there is a charge. The fact that a number of datasets need to be pooled to obtain reasonable sample sizes for minority ethnic groups and that the level of geography does not offer information about local labour markets makes it unfriendly data for use in employers' monitoring of equal opportunities.

Census data on the whole population is available from the Office for National Statistics (ONS) website (www.ons.gov.uk), from the General Register Office for Scotland and from the Northern Ireland Research Agency. Where finer breakdowns or different tables than are offered are required, customised tables have to be ordered and purchased from ONS. There can be a lengthy wait to get ordered data. For example, this project ordered customised tables, which had still not arrived 11 months from submitting our order.[2] The cost per table is estimated as being around £50. The delay in the supply of customised tables is likely to be considerably reduced as the data ages and the backlog of orders subsides.

The SARs from the 2001 Census were expected to be available for use as part of this project and it seemed to offer the best access for employers wanting to do monitoring. It was expected to provide individual microdata on 3 per cent of the UK population with all of the necessary individual characteristics available and accessible, and the potential to define local labour market areas based on local authorities. However, changes in confidentiality requirements and disclosure control led to long delays in 2001 SAR data being made available to researchers and to reductions in the level of detail. This included reducing the geographical detail on the SAR data, as compared with 1991 SAR data. This was a major blow to this project. It was, by implication, also a major blow to the prospect that employers, across a range of businesses and local labour market recruitments areas, would be able to access data they would need to make workforce equal opportunities monitoring more effective than was previously possible. The implications of this change of access to SAR microdata and level of geography were very serious for this and many other projects.

It is still possible for this report to illustrate the method by which employers can use external data as part of their monitoring of equal opportunities. However, without changes in the ONS data-release policies, or a new service for employers being set up, it would not be possible for employers to get direct access to data that can be easily customised to their needs.

The contents of each dataset and the illustrative sample sizes described above are based on the controlled access microdata samples accessed at ONS Titchfield under conditions of high security.

Comparisons with the USA Census data

Again, the contrast between data available in the UK and that available in the USA is striking. In the USA, the provision of Census data to employers, software to make it accessible in the format employers need and software to carry out the analyses are all provided by private sector initiatives.

Four government departments paid approximately $1 million to the Census Bureau in the late 1990s to purchase a raw datafile suitable for use in monitoring affirmative action. The data is based on adults over 18 in the labour force at the Census. These four departments have given a private company, EEO Visions, without charge, a copy of the raw data with a view to it providing a software front-end it can sell. The software makes the data more accessible to government users and to any private company that wants to buy it.

The software allows tabulations based on aggregate data for 475 occupational groups and areas with over 50,000 residents. It offers a population breakdown of such areas by ethnic origin, gender and qualification levels (based on the 2000 USA Census categories) by spatial area, as well as the other variables listed below. The tabular reports are in a format suitable to feed into the AAP external availability assessment process. Other specialist HR database software products have been devised into which the Census data is loaded, in order to produce the necessary workforce analyses.

The software is a menu-driven product that refers to Census variables. The main menus are as follows.

1 *Workplace-based*: choice of residence- or workplace-based data on employee location/geography.

2 *Format*: (this is an option related to the number of minority ethnic groupings).

3 *Geography*: tables are available for each state, metro, county or city areas with 50,000 adults aged 18+. There is also a look-up option table from this window where you can type the name of the place (a smaller place) and find the bigger unit it is a part of; sometimes more than one option is offered.

4 *Detailed occupations*: this is a list of occupations in nested layers; 23 standard occupational coding (SOC codes) on the top level with each breaking out (if clicked) into sub-groups and ultimately to the 477 of the possible 509 three-digit occupation codes. Again, there is look-up table where a more detailed occupation can be typed in and it will then indicate the three-digit code (and higher codes) the occupation is part of.

5 *Industry codes*: this is an 88-category standard industry code (SIC) classification. This also has a look-up option for you to type in a more detailed industry and find its higher-level group.

6 *Earnings*: this is ten (or eight) earnings bands based on 1999 earnings values banded from the Census and provided with the data (not alterable).

7 *Age*: this is a set of age groups (four in all) covering the post-18 workforce.

8 *Education*: this is a set of five broad highest education groups.

There is a facility in the software to define job groups, and to weight the component jobs that make up the group (e.g. 20:20:60 if three groups) and provide a weighted report of the number of minorities or women in that job group. The software can also export the report to Excel software.

This set of variables will, in principle, enable companies to define fairly narrow job groupings – for example, lawyers with higher degree (e.g. MBA) paid in top income bracket – and find the minority and gender populations in this category (which might be very low or even non-existent).

The data provided by EEO Visions does not include disability status or addresses. It has already been coded into geography and this is fixed, as are the earnings bands.

EEO-1 reports and sets of categories

In addition to the nine-category occupations for reporting in the EEO-1 report for private sector companies, there are two other sets of occupations.

1   EEO-4: this set applies to federal and state government jobs.

2   EEO-6: this set applies to higher education organisations.

There was also a 'find' option on the USA Government's 'Equal Opportunities' website for the 1990 Census data. Here you can ask online for a statistic defined in the way you want it and receive it online.

Total minorities versus finer breakdowns

There is a difference of opinion between government agencies over whether AAPs should be conducted using 'total minorities' or separate minority ethnic groups. The Equal Employment Opportunity Commission (EEOC) does not like the use of 'total minorities' but the Department of Labor thinks this should be allowed for simplicity.

Workforce definitions

Since the USA population Census data used for affirmative action monitoring contains a range of characteristics about the individuals, it is possible to use some fairly fine-tuned definitions. A list of possible workforce groups that could be studied using the USA Census in equal opportunities monitoring is provided below (Box 14).

Box 14 Examples of work groups possible to analyse with USA 2000 Census data

The sizes of these population groups can be obtained broken down by either gender or minority ethnic origin for an area of 50,000 or more residents:

- environmental engineers with a master's degree

- cost estimators with a bachelor's degree

- general and operations managers with earnings $75,000–124,999 per annum

- marketing sales managers in pharmaceuticals industry

- news analysts, reporters and correspondents aged 40 and over

- compliance officers (except agriculture, construction or health and safety) with earnings $125,000 or more per annum.

Conclusions

This project charted the data available in the UK that might be useful to employers. The lack of clear and easily available geographical identifiers for labour market areas in surveys with sufficiently large sample sizes is one important constraint. As we saw earlier in Chapter 2, employers who collect data were not all using Census categories for recording the minority ethnic identity of their applicants or employees. This too will restrict the ability to match Census to workforce data. The suggestion that organisations be encouraged to deviate from Census ethnic identity categories in at least one race equality document would, if enacted, restrict the ability to use official data in monitoring. It would mean that comparisons of statistics from official sources to employers' data would be able to take place only when all minority ethnic groups were collapsed into one category.

4 Case study illustrations of monitoring statistics in the UK

Introduction

Below we offer a series of illustrations from our organisation case studies of how UK Census data could be used in the monitoring of organisations' equal opportunities policies. These cases have been selected in order to provide illustrations across different types of equality issue, a range of vacancies, job criteria and different spatial areas over which recruitment takes place.

Illustrations

Illustration 1: Energise

Case of technical staff (mainly professional and science engineers) and gender applicant profile.

Background

The organisation is an international manufacturer, which has over 100 centres worldwide. Because of the associated nature of some of its businesses, it was not able to give figures for the total employees across the global business.

Workforce composition 2001–02

The organisation was in the process of creating a central database and reviewing all its recruitment methodologies.

Recruitment

The organisation has an extensive graduate recruitment programme. After passing in-house tests, graduates are attached to particular business units. Experienced recruitment is a new and growing area for the organisation. For these posts, there are job specifications but initial application is by CV. The organisation has set targets in relation to both gender and ethnicity for 2008. The organisation mainly uses European Union legal frameworks for recruitment but, where necessary, adapts to the particular country of operation.

With respect to geography, posts are advertised nationally and internationally through specialist press and via the company's website. In some instances, local staff are taken on through agencies. The employer uses specialist agencies for part of its human resources function.

Analysis for gender

Figure 3 presents some recruitment data from Energise for Technical staff in 2003–04 with 2001 UK Census microdata (SAR) compared (figures in Appendix Table A3.1).

Figure 3 Energise technical staff recruitment figures 2003–04 and 2001 and SAR 2001 Census data for given populations (per cent women in specified categories)

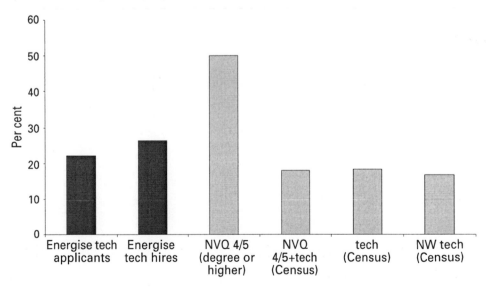

Source: Census 2001 controlled access microdata 3 per cent sample. Qualification levels differ in Scotland and are provided separately in the SAR data and not included here. Age 20–59.
NW: North West region only.
NVQ 4/5: highest qualification levels NVQ levels 4 or 5.
Tech: technical occupations defined from SAR as SOC minor codes 211, 212 and 311.
Figures contained in Appendix Table A3.1.

As Figure 3 shows, the 2001 Census reveals that, nationally in 2001, women were approximately 50 per cent of the workforce with a degree level or above, but only 17.9 per cent of the population with an engineering or science job and a degree or higher qualification across England, Wales and Northern Ireland. The figure is 16.8 per cent if the area is restricted to the North West region where part of Energise was located. Energise was getting 22.1 per cent of its applicants for these technical jobs from women. Energise seems to be doing better than would be expected on the basis of the pool of women qualified to do its jobs.

When the hires are examined, 26.4 per cent were women. Given that they applied, women had a 1.9 per cent chance of being hired by Energise compared with a 1.5 per cent chance for men. These are small differences but Energise is gradually tackling the imbalance of women in its workforce.

Energise has been setting targets for gender and ethnicity. These figures suggest Energise's strategy to build up a more mixed-gender workforce is proving successful. The Census figures also show it needs to recruit outside of the local North West area if it is to continue to be successful, since there is a lower proportion of this type of workforce in the North West compared with nationally. In the longer term, it may want to work with training providers in the area to address the skills shortages. For example, it may be possible for employers to work with Regional Development Agencies to devise new routes into engineering occupations.

Illustration 2: NorthLA

Case of senior manager job and gender workforce profile.

Background

NorthLA is a public sector service provider. It employs approximately 23,000 people across a number of offices in Northern England.

Workforce composition

The staff in 2000 were 71.8 per cent male, 11.9 per cent minority ethnic and 2.3 per cent disabled.

Recruitment

Recruitment is under the immediate control of a particular line manager and advertised in the in-house jobs bulletin, or in the local\national press, or, for senior skilled posts, in specialist trade press. There is some variation in relation to job type, for example, it differs in the organisation's call centre where recruitment is more casual. All vacancies have a person-requirement form and some jobs require professional qualifications. Senior-post recruitment is sometimes assisted by an agency. For this example, we take a senior manager job in NorthLA.

Analysis by gender

The workforce figures of NorthLA are set out in Figure 4 for the year 2000 (figures in Appendix Table A3.2).

Figure 4 NorthLA female workforce figures 2000 in senior manager posts and SAR 2001 Census data for given populations (per cent women in specified categories)

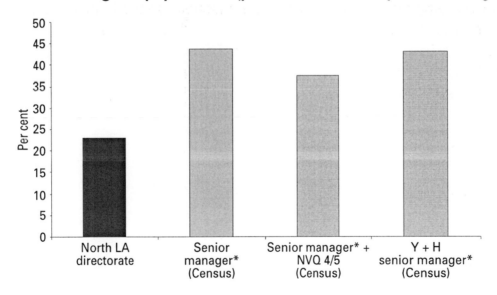

Source: Census 2001 controlled access microdata 3 per cent sample. Qualification levels differ in Scotland and are provided separately in the SAR data and not included here. Age 20–59.
Y + H: Yorkshire and Humberside region only.
NVQ 4/5: highest qualification levels NVQ levels 4 or 5.
* SAR data includes SOC minor codes 113, 114, 117, 118, 122, 123, 244, 245.
Figures contained in Appendix Table A3.2.

NorthLA has relatively few workers at this senior management grade (216 in 2000) and it becomes more difficult to match the qualifications required for this job to the Census categories. At this grade, 23.1 per cent of managers were women. The national population of senior managers who work in public sector organisations similar to NorthLA consists of 43.8 per cent of women when measured by their occupation alone. The proportion of women with these occupations in the North region is similar to the national figure. Adding in the criteria that these managers need to have a degree-level qualification reduces the proportion of qualified female applicants nationally to 37.4 per cent.

These Census figures for the percentages of qualified workers in such jobs are all higher than the proportion of women NorthLA employs at this grade. It is possible that the match is not precise enough to be sure we are comparing like with like. It would be possible to consider the Census pool after adding in an age criterion (e.g. above 35) for this post and this may reduce the proportion of women in the pool who were qualified for the post. Other than that it is unlikely that the Census data will give us any closer approximation to identifying the qualified pool. However, on the basis of these statistics, NorthLA needs to give consideration to its recruitment and promotion of women to see whether there are gender biases in any of the procedures.

Illustration 3: PublicServ

Case of support staff recruitment in local area and ethnic applicant profile.

Background

PublicServ is a public sector service provider. It employs approximately 10,000 employees across a number of offices in Greater Manchester. Of these around 7,000 are service provider staff and 3,000 are support staff.

Workforce composition

The support staff in 2000–01 were composed of 35 per cent male, 2.6 per cent minority ethnic and 4.2 per cent disabled employees.

Recruitment

On average, PublicServ recruits approximately 500 new support staff per year. For a new post, a proposal is written by the particular line manager and decided on by a personnel panel. The small minority of senior support vacancies are advertised in the national press and specialist publications.

For this example, we take the lower-/medium-grade levels of support staff that are equivalent to NVQ levels 2 and 3. A selection of advertisements for such jobs in 2003 is displayed in Boxes 15 to 17 below. The actual wording of the advertisements is used but the identity of the employer has been disguised.

Support staff vacancies at this level are advertised locally using the regional and local press and internally within the organisation. The organisation also advertises in local libraries and on its website. A substantial amount of recruitment has been devolved down to specific offices.

Box 15 Administrative assistant

... to provide general administrative, clerical and technical support to other staff. You will attend meetings and take notes and produce minutes as required, analyse information and produce statistical data, creating spreadsheets where necessary.

Possessing excellent keyboard skills you will access computer databases to obtain information and update records, and you will undertake routine office tasks such as photocopying, answering the telephone and dealing with enquiries.

Previous administrative experience, a flexible approach to workloads, good communication skills and the ability to work on your own initiative are also required for this post.

£11,634–£13,251 p.a.

Box 16 Researcher

... you will collate, research, evaluate and disseminate information retrieved from a variety of sources.

You will provide an objective and structured research support function to the group and use additional sources to enhance the quality of information available. To be successful in this post, you must be able to undertake data retrieval, analysis and evaluation using a variety of sources.

A knowledge of computer applications including databases and spreadsheets coupled with excellent written and verbal communication skills are essential for this role.

£13,563–£14,487

Box 17 Clerk/word processor (job share)

... you will provide administrative support and word processing service to the members of a group.

Previous word processing experience is essential as you will type reports, briefing papers, memoranda, letters and minutes from meetings. Excellent communication skills are required as you will be dealing with the public and commercial organisations in person and on the telephone.

Shortlisted applicants will be required to attend for a typing test and will need to achieve the required standard to proceed.

£11,634–£13,251 p.a.

Analysis by ethnicity

Figure 5 presents one year's recruitment figures for support staff in office O5 of this organisation (see Appendix Table A3.3 for values).

Figure 5 PublicServ minority ethnic support staff recruitment (office O5) at NVQ levels 2 + 3 and SAR 2001 Census statistics for minorities in Greater Manchester (GM) and sub-GM area for given populations (per cent minorities in specified categories)

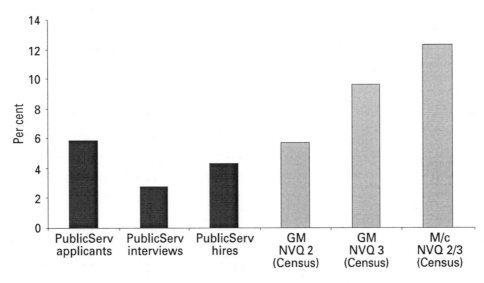

Source: Census 2001 controlled access microdata 3 per cent sample. Qualification levels differ in Scotland and are provided separately in the SAR data and not included here. Age 20–59.
GM: Greater Manchester area only.
M/c: Trafford, Salford and Manchester areas only are from published tables on ONS website for population of all ages 16–74.
NVQ 2/3: highest qualification levels NVQ levels 2 or 3.
Minorities covers major 2001 Census groupings of mixed, all Asian or Asian British, black Caribbean, black African, Chinese and other ethnic groups.
Figures contained in Appendix Table A3.3.

Over the year, 1,446 applications were received for the type of support-staff posts shown in this example, of which 86 applicants were from the local minority ethnic populations. This gives a percentage application rate from minority ethnic groups of 5.9 per cent.[1] Across all of the office departments of this organisation, for support-staff job vacancies, 6.3 per cent of applications came from the minority ethnic population. These applicants' figures are low compared with the Census-based minority ethnic share of the local population, which is 8.8 per cent for Greater Manchester and even higher at 12.3 per cent for a selection of three Greater Manchester districts. However, when compared with statistics for Greater Manchester broken down by NVQ level, then section O5 is gaining applicants for support jobs at NVQ level 2 from the population in proportion to their ethnic diversity. Also, support jobs across the organisation are getting an above-average mix of minority ethnic populations. However, applicants for support jobs at NVQ level 3 are lower from the local minority ethnic populations than might be expected. Ideally, we would like to get the same data broken down by NVQ level for the three central Greater Manchester districts to have a closer match to the likely local labour market recruitment area for these types of support jobs. But the sample sizes in the SAR data begin to get too small for such analyses.

Not surprisingly, Greater Manchester as a whole has a share of minority ethnic to total population that is smaller than the same share in its more central districts. This difference in minority ethnic share of the total local population highlights how important it is to map the geography of the recruitment area for any particular job type as closely as possible to the area for which the statistics are produced.

The applications can also vary across sections of an organisation. Decisions about the level of breakdown, whether at the level of the whole organisation or a sub-section of it, will rely on there being reasonable sizes of applications over a given time period. It will often be necessary to aggregate across sections or departments of the organisation and take applications over a year in order to provide sufficient sample sizes for analysis.

We judged from the job descriptions that the appropriate target population for the vast majority of support-staff jobs advertised by this employer was individuals of working age with NVQ level 2 or 3. Because of the location of the employer's workplace, applicants would most likely be living in three central districts of Greater Manchester. These support-staff jobs were at pay levels where it would not be expected that applicants would travel long distances or pay for such travel. The employer's database usefully allows analysis throughout the recruitment process. Out of the total 1,446 applications to office O5, 393 were given interviews. This is a rate of 27.2 per cent, although lower at 12.8 per cent (11 of 86) in the case of minority ethnic applicants who received an interview. Of those 393 candidates interviewed, 17.8 per cent were appointed and the figure was 18.2 per cent for minority ethnic interviewees.

Across the whole organisation, the figures vary from office O5 to some extent. Overall, of the 7,476 applicants who applied for support staff jobs over the year, 26.7 per cent were given an interview (n = 1,999). The equivalent figure for minority ethnic applicants was 17.8 per cent, better overall than the performance of office O5. Of all those interviewed, 24.5 per cent were appointed, compared with 19 per cent of minority ethnic interviewees who were appointed.

How should the organisation view these figures? Clearly, PublicServ is probably getting fewer applicants from minority ethnic candidates for support jobs at NVQ level 3 than it might reasonably expect given the qualified population locally. Its internal recruitment decisions about interviews for applicants suggest that minority ethnic applicants are less likely than the population as a whole to obtain an interview, but, having got an interview, minority ethnic interviewees are slightly more likely than other interviewees to be appointed to a support job in office O5. However, this finding did not apply across the organisation as a whole.

The employer's collection and analysis of such data allows assessment and modification of its recruitment practices. The data suggests that this organisation needs to continue to review its recruitment advertising, its image within the minority ethnic population and its internal decision making about offering interviews and offering jobs to applicants to make sure there is no bias against minority ethnic candidates in all of its departments.

Illustration 4: NorthLA

A case of senior manager job by workforce ethnic profile.

For this example, we take an experienced regeneration officer to have at least a degree-level qualification in NorthLA, the public services provider whose profile was described above in Illustration 2. An example of an advertisement for such jobs is displayed below (Box 18). The actual wording of the advertisements is used but the identity of the employer has been disguised.

> **Box 18 Advertisement for a regeneration officer**
>
> £23,235–£25,035 p.a.
>
> We are looking for a Regeneration Projects Officer.
>
> You will need three years' experience of project development; a degree or equivalent qualification; knowledge of SRB programmes and other grant regimes and knowledge of computerised information systems.

Analysis by ethnicity

The proportion of minority ethnic employees working as senior managers in NorthLA in 2000 was 12.6 per cent (Figure 6); values are in Appendix Table 3.4. This is a higher proportion of minorities than the national average in senior management jobs in local government, which, according to the SAR Census, was 7.4 per cent for all managers and 9.2 per cent if managers had a degree or higher qualification. The region had well below the national average of minorities in its population of senior managers (5.6 per cent). This is not surprising, since minority ethnic populations are known to cluster in a number of urban conurbations. When statistics for region populations are provided, this reduces the percentage of minorities by adding larger numbers of rural dwellers (mostly non-minorities) to the denominator.

Figure 6 Minority ethnic workforce statistics for NorthLA in 2000 and 2001 and SAR 2001 Census data for England for given populations (per cent of minorities in specified categories)

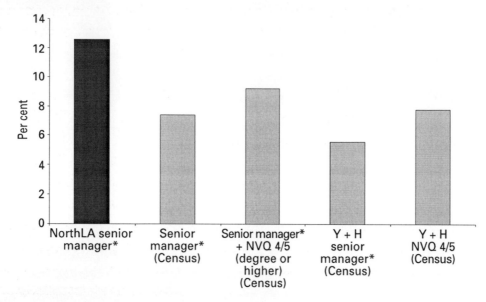

Source: Census 2001 controlled access microdata 3 per cent sample. Age 20–59.
Minorities covers major 2001 Census groupings of mixed, all Asian or Asian British, black Caribbean, black African, Chinese and other ethnic groups.
Y + H: Yorkshire and Humberside region only.
* In SAR data, this includes SOC minor codes 111, 113, 114, 117, 118, 122, 123, 243, 244, 245.
Figures contained in Appendix Table A3.4.

This is a case where more local geography for the particular urban conurbation would be helpful. However, from the SAR data, such finer levels of geography do not offer the potential to do SOC and qualification-level analyses simultaneously because of small sample sizes.

These figures suggest that NorthLA is doing well at getting a diverse workforce that represents the local area population and even at higher-grade occupations.

Illustration 5: ED-SE

A case of academic jobs by applicant ethnic profile.

Recruitment

This is the case of a higher education institution located in the South East of England. All vacancies for academic posts are advertised in specialist press at the national, and occasionally international, level. Applicants would be expected to need a degree and publications to be eligible for these jobs.

Whether applicants have publications is not available in the Census data or usually in any other large-scale, official, general survey. The closest approximation, therefore, to the qualifications required would be having a higher degree. In the SAR data, first and higher degrees are aggregated into one category, so it is not possible to distinguish very accurately the population who will be eligible and qualified to apply for an academic post in a higher education institution. It is possible to know the SOC category that characterises employed individuals' current employment, and this gives another indicator of the qualified population. However, this too has its limitations in the SOC minor three-digit categories. The categories in question indicate 'professional teachers' and 'professional researchers'. It would be possible to identify populations in these categories who had a degree qualification or above. However, it is clear that school teachers also end up in the 'professional teachers' category. So, again, the match is not very precise.

As far as the geography is concerned, such posts would be expected to be recruited from a national labour market, rather than being restricted to the South East. However, housing costs in the South East are a barrier to applicants living in other areas applying or relocating.

Analysis by ethnicity

The figures in Tables 3–5 show the applicants, shortlisted and appointments to academic posts in one higher education institution in the South East. Although white academics predominate in the applications to ED-SE, compared with the workforce nationally who are qualified to degree and above level, ED-SE has a more diverse set of applicants than the closest national qualified population; only 75.7 per cent of ED-SE's applicants were white compared with a population of qualified people of over 90 per cent white. As far as it is possible to tell, ED-SE is attracting a diverse set of applicants. However, as mentioned above, the comparison group from the Census is not ideal, since it is not sufficiently well defined for the qualifications required to do this type of job.

Table 3 Recruitment figures to academic posts at ED-SE compared with 2001 Census employed workforce statistics (individual SAR 3 per cent sample)

Applicants**	ED-SE academic posts 2001–03	2001 Census EWN SOC** 20–60	2001 Census EWN NVQ 4+5 20–60	2001 Census EWN SOC**+ NVQ 4/5 20–60
White	75.7	92.4	90.8	92.5
Black	8.5	1.9	2.4	1.8
Asian	13.2	3.4	4.3	3.4
Mixed	2.6	1.0	1.0	0.9
Other		1.4	1.4	1.4
Total %	100	100	100	100
N	1,844	42,964	22,965	36,691

Source: 2001 individual SAR 3 per cent sample.
* Categories used in organisations' reporting of figures.
** Closest match SOC codes are 231, 232 and 242.
EWN: England, Wales and Northern Ireland.

Table 4 Percentage who get shortlisted given they apply

Shortlisted	%	N
White	29.0	1,396
Black	14.6	157
Asian	16.0	243
Mixed	33.3	48

Table 5 Percentage who get appointed given they get shortlisted

Appointments	%	N
White	32.6	405
Black	13.0	23
Asian	10.3	39
Mixed	25.0	16

An analysis of candidates' progress through the recruitment procedure suggests that the organisation may have some bias in its procedures. Whereas white applicants have a 29 per cent chance of being shortlisted and a 32.6 per cent chance of being appointed, given they were on the shortlist, applicants from other ethnic groups generally have much lower chances. Applicants of mixed ethnic origin group are an exception in that their chances of being shortlisted, given they applied, are higher than for applicants in all other groups including white applicants. However, the mixed ethnic origin group is the smallest in size and this needs to be noted.

For ED-SE, its recruitment procedures and image are attracting a diverse set of candidates for academic posts, but its internal procedures during appointment need a review. It may be that a bias against ethnic minorities is part of the way appointment panels judge candidates for academic jobs at ED-SE. However, there is another possible explanation. It is possible that ED-SE's attempt to attract this diverse set of applicants is producing a higher proportion of unsuitable candidates, which gets reflected in their lower chances of being shortlisted. However, a key feature of these statistics that needs considering within the organisation is that, once shortlisted, candidates from minority groups are less likely to be appointed.

Illustration 6: Transit

Case of manager-level post with degree restricted to local labour market by ethnic workforce profile.

Background

This employer is a private/public employer and has approximately 12,000 employees plus some additional employees in sister companies.

Workforce composition

The staff in 2003 were composed of 82.6 per cent male and 31.8 per cent minority ethnic origin. No data were available on the number of staff with disabilities.

Recruitment

Recruitment to lower-grade jobs (for example, customer services assistants) uses local advertising including local press and the job centre in addition to the website. Local recruitment is important because of the unsocial hours involved in many of Transit's jobs. Manager jobs would be advertised nationally in the national press and in specialist journals. An example advertisement for such jobs is displayed below (Box 19). The actual wording of the advertisements is used but the identity of the employer has been disguised.

> ### Box 19 Human factors specialist
>
> Fixed-term contract 18 months
>
> Up to £35,000 plus benefits
>
> A Human Factors Specialist to the Risk Assessment Development Team is required. You should combine a relevant degree or equivalent with applied experience. You will need to be flexible and adaptable in your approach to the role and must possess the ability to liaise effectively with safety, operational and engineering managers and staff of all levels. You must also have good numerical and verbal reasoning skills.

Each job has a person-job specification and some require professional qualifications. For some posts, qualifications are less important than others. For example, for some posts, applicants are tested for concentration and alertness skills. They can also be examined in role-plays as well as interviews. The manager interviewed suggested that:

> … qualifications are not the best judge of a good candidate for many posts and an emphasis on qualifications could work against equal opportunities.

For certain posts, there are, however, minimum qualifications.

The employer has at present a number of initiatives to recruit more women to all jobs and more ethnic minorities to senior posts. It has a number of recruitment targets for 2006, which have been agreed with the trade union.

Analysis by ethnicity

For this example, we consider a risk assessment safety manager vacancy requiring a degree-level qualification. Of the total management staff of 286, 30 per cent were of black or minority ethnic origin. This compares with the minority ethnic population in Inner London making up 23.9 per cent of 20–60 year olds with NVQ 4 or 5 according to the 2001 Census.

In this respect, the organisation is recruiting at rates above the local qualified pool. However, no members of the senior management team were from minority ethnic populations. It is perhaps not surprising to hear that the organisation has been putting effort into recruiting and promoting minority ethnic employees.

The organisation examines the ethnicity and gender of applicants at the different stages of recruitment (applicant stage, shortlisting and appointment). It analyses these statistics where there is a substantial number (e.g. 100) to see if ethnicity or gender are a factor. The manager interviewed was also aware of the issues relating to the significance of statistical differences (confidence intervals and standard deviations). The organisation has adjusted some aspects of the recruitment process where problems were identified, including training for recruiters and in certain recruitment tests where there was 'thought to be adverse racial and gender impact'.

This employer sets targets in liaison with the unions. There are 32 such targets for 2006. These are long-term goals. According to the manager interviewed, there is 'gross under-representation of women across all sectors and of BME [black and minority ethnic] groups in senior posts'. However, employment of minority ethnic groups at lower grades was considered 'good' with one-third of the workforce from a minority ethnic population, although at a senior level this was only 16 per cent. The manager went on to say:

> … they need to look at engineering and law. They have made presentations at both these professions' national bodies. They have a gender equality programme … it is a very difficult working environment for women.

The organisation had also done some ad hoc profiling of the wider community but felt it needed more information in relation to gender and ethnicity and education/skills.

Illustration 7: various employers

Cases of various jobs in local labour markets by workforce disability profile.

Under the Disability Discrimination Act, disability is defined as:

> … a physical or mental impairment which has a substantial and long-term adverse effect on a person's ability to carry out normal day-to-day activities.

The definition covers impairments affecting the senses such as sight and hearing, and mental impairments including learning difficulties and mental health.

Hirst *et al.* (2004) in their review of the employment of disabled people in the public sector state that, in their research, there was no uniformity in how disabled people was defined. As has been argued by Burchardt (2004), a broad definition of disability in a survey can suggest disability is more widespread and can also lead to underestimating the barriers facing those with severe disabilities.

Using this type of analysis for investigating organisations' recruitment of disabled people comes up against the low sample sizes of disabled people in all large-scale surveys and the problems of defining disability. As reviewed in Chapter 3, the Census is not very good at measuring disabled status. The Labour Force Survey is better, but has the problems of small sample sizes. There is the additional problem of whether all disabled people should be included in the analysis, given that some of them will not wish to be considered for employment. It is difficult, therefore, to define or identify from survey data the true population measure for these analyses. This is an area needing more thought and possibly some refinement in the survey questions.

Here we present some of the case study data across a range of organisations that gave us data on the extent of their recruitment of disabled people (Table 6) in comparison with the extent of this population in the LFS data (Table 7). Disabled people in LFS are presented in two groups: either they have a DDA disability; or they say they have a work-limiting disability, but may not necessarily be DDA disabled. We have excluded any people with a DDA or work-limiting disability who said they did not want to work. Failure to exclude this group considerably increases the percentages of people with either of these disability statuses to almost double in some cases.

It is clear that all of the organisations for which we could collect data are managing to recruit only very small proportions of disabled people. As shown above, one of these organisations, PublicServ, gave us data on their numbers of disabled people as they passed through the recruitment process. Disabled applicants for support-staff jobs constituted 1.5 per cent of a year's applicants and 1 per cent of appointees. Disabled people who applied had a 24 per cent chance of being interviewed compared with a similar 26 per cent chance for all applicants, but a 17 per cent chance of being appointed given they were interviewed compared with the 24 per cent chance in the case of all applicants. These figures suggest that the organisation needs to consider the appointment stage of its recruitment procedures for potential bias against disabled people.

Table 6 Disabled people in the workforce of case study organisations

Organisation and type of job	% applicants who were disabled people/year	% workforce who were disabled people
PublicServ 2002		
Support staff (NVQ 2/3)	1.6 (*n* = 7,476)	
All staff		
ED-NW 2002		
Admin. staff		1.0 (*n* = *)
All staff		0.1 (*n* = 6,600)
NorthLA		
Clerical NVQ 2		3.1 (*n* = 4,413)
Senior managers NVQ 4/5		3.1 (*n* = 1,790)
Teachers		1.3 (*n* = 4,631)
Transit		
Safety manager		0.0 (*n* = 37)

* *Figure came from case interview but* n *value not available.*

Table 7 LFS figures on disabled who want to work (ages 16–60), spring LFS 2003, weighted percentages

Population	Disability Discrimination Act (DDA)*	Work-limiting illness (can include DDA)*	Unweighted *n*
UK			
Total	10.4	6.6	73,762
NVQ 2 + 3	10.2	6.9	34,544
North West region			
Total	10.8	6.3	5,465
NVQ 2+3	10.8	6.9	2,802
Greater Manchester			
Total	11.3	6.3	2,592
NVQ 2 + 3	11.1	7.1	1,333

* *Excludes disabled people who were not working who said they did not want a job.*

Statistical tools for assessing the significance of differences in recruitment

It is important to consider whether differences in application and appointment rates for different groups are statistically significant or whether they may have occurred by chance. In the USA, employers are required to assess whether a difference is significant using one of three methods. This then defines whether there is evidence, using USA terminology, of 'adverse impact' or underutilisation in the organisation's workforce of a particular minority group. The three tests used are as follows: the four-fifths rule, the standard deviation rule and the 0.05 level of significance. More details of how these calculations are carried out are provided in Appendix 4.

5 Discussion and conclusions

Main findings

This project has highlighted a number of conclusions about equal opportunities and their implementation by UK employers. Many organisations have adopted equal opportunities policies but have not moved forward in their monitoring to even a basic level, either because they do not collect necessary data or because they do not analyse the data they collect on their workforce and applicants.

After 30 years of legislation, many employers still do not have a profile of their workforce and job applicants broken down by gender or race. The employers we examined were all large employers, all considering themselves to have a commitment to being equal opportunities employers. In this sense, our findings agree with those of Hoque and Noon (2001) that few employers have put systems in place to ensure equal opportunities in practice, although they claim equal opportunities in written statements and advertisements. There was evidence that public sector organisations were moving towards the goal of better data collection and analysis of their workforce as part of equal opportunity monitoring at the time of our fieldwork interviews. Data collection and analysis of applicant data was still weak in a number of these public sector organisations. Private sector organisations were on the whole well behind those in the public sector in collecting data on their workforce and applicants.

All employers were faced with problems of incomplete data, especially on classifying employees' ethnic origin and disability. None had complete data and none had clear strategies for dealing with the incompleteness of their employee or applicant data. The employers studied did not commit anything approaching the level of human resources to data collection or monitoring that is standard in similar organisations in the USA.

The 2001 UK Census data could be useful in monitoring both employee profiles and applicants' data, especially for discrimination by gender or ethnic origin. This project illustrated the potential of this new data through a number of illustrations. However, there were problems in accessing the data, which would need to be overcome before this could be a useful tool for employers. On the basis of current access to 2001 Census data, there are many barriers to employers using the data in assisting their EO monitoring. Employers will need clear guidance on how to monitor effectively as well as access to clear and easy-to-read tables in order to make comparisons with relevant qualified populations. The Labour Force Survey is slightly better than the Census in terms of the questions and categories it uses to identify disabled people and their ability to work, but it is not perfect. Also, the LFS sample sizes for analyses of disabled people are very small.

Using such data in monitoring does not guarantee to show that discrimination is absent or present. It does, however, raise questions about organisations' policies and can direct attention to the areas of their practice they need to consider in more detail. The method of monitoring illustrated here also has the potential to be used in other applications – for example, UCAS applications for students' applications to higher education.

Recommendations

1   *Data collection* : there is a need to upgrade data collected by employers relevant to monitoring equal opportunities. This is the first step in being able to monitor. Employers should record and enter into their databases the following information about applicants to jobs and employees: gender, ethnic identity, age, disability, location of residence, highest qualification and occupation or job vacancy. For applicants only, they should include whether shortlisted and whether appointed. Without this step, progress on monitoring cannot be made. One option is for government to require all employers to collect and record data on the gender, ethnic origin and disability status of their employees and applicants for jobs, as a minimum. The list could be extended to other equality issues in due course – for example, age and religion. Legislation about data collection in the USA underpins the monitoring and affirmative action plans as well as making organisations commit resources to collecting and analysing the data. The current requirement for public sector organisations to collect data for monitoring the ethnic identity of their employees thus needs extending to include the other equality issues and across all UK organisations.

2   *Data collection categories* : the ability to compare statistics from official data sources with employers' data rests on both using the same categories. This report recommends that employers stick to or move to using official Census categories, especially for ethnic identity, which is probably the set of categories most disputed.

3   *Missing data* : government needs to issue guidelines on how best to handle missing data on employees' and applicants' ethnic origin or disability status. Ideally, it should make it a requirement of entry to the workforce of any public or

private organisation that the individual provide such data about themselves. This may require additional legislation to effect. It would take the onus off the employer to have to worry about obtaining complete information. The advantage of making it mandatory is that more accurate classifications of the workforce and applicants would then be available to carry out monitoring. Failing that, clearer guidance about what are acceptable levels of missing data needs to be issued and about what to do where below-acceptable levels apply.

4 *Access to Census data* : access to Census data for employers needs to be made easier. In principle, it would be possible to follow the example of the USA in this respect. Offers of single statistics through website requests would be possible through ONS or a contracted body. Similarly, access to a form of SAR data could be made, through software that helped and guided employers to find the statistics closest to their own workforce profile or job-specification criteria. Packages like CASOC, which match a written-text occupation to the closest occupation SOC code, are already available. This could be incorporated into such software. Alternatively, Regional Development Agencies (RDAs) might be able to provide all the statistics possible for SOC by NVQ for gender, ethnic origin and disability populations for the local travel-to-work areas in the region and put these on a website.

5 *Good affordable monitoring software* : this will help employers carry out their monitoring by (a) providing relevant Census data and (b) linked software to carry out workforce and applicant comparisons of the type that are easily available in the USA.

6 *Local area statistics* : the trend to provide fewer and fewer local area statistics because of the risks of disclosure about individuals inhibits the use of microdata like that contained in the SAR data for the purpose of employers' monitoring. The use of Census data in the USA has got round these problems by aggregating data to certain levels in the software. It would be possible to adopt a similar approach in the UK. But, equally, providing the full list of possible report breakdowns through RDAs for each area (below region level) would be an alternative approach.

7 *Monitoring on disability* : further development needs to take place of the questions and categories in the Census data to identify disabled people who have the capacity to take up employment.

Best practice

Employers who want to achieve best practice in equal opportunities monitoring need to carry out the following steps.

1 Have an equal opportunities form given out to all applicants for jobs (web-based as well as more traditional channels). Applicants need to be strongly encouraged to fill in this form. However, they can be assured that the information provided will remain totally confidential and will not be used at any stage of the recruitment process.

2 Information collected from the EO applicants' form needs to be computerised. Each applicant's record needs to be updated with whether or not they get shortlisted, whether or not they get interviewed, and whether they were offered a job (and accepted it).

3 Annual printouts of applicants shortlisted and interviewees' characteristics by type of job should be produced from the database.

4 These statistics can be compared with Census data where it is available, along the lines shown in the example illustrations in this report. This will help to identify where under-representation may be occurring.

5 Databases of employees should include the important equal opportunity characteristics. If providing this information is made mandatory at the point of entry to the organisation, this will enable a complete record for each individual for gender and ethnic identity to be kept.

6 Regular profiles of the workforce should be produced and examined and compared with Census data on the populations of the appropriate pool of workers with such skills to see where under-representation may be occurring. It is also in the interests of employers to have such datasets in relation to any legal cases that are brought concerning discrimination on the grounds of gender, ethnicity, age or disability.

7 The statistics on applicants and the workforce should be examined by personnel, human resource directors or equal opportunities directors and trade unions or employees' representatives. Where there appears to be under-representation, the organisation needs to consider whether it is has already done all it can to widen its recruitment. It should also seek information from other best-practice employers about innovations in recruitment appropriate for particular groups.

8   Management at the top level of the organisation should see these statistics and discuss their implications as well as any action plan and follow-up that ensues.

9   An action plan should be drawn up where under-representation is found for any particular group. The statistics and action plan need to be seen and approved by the business unit manager and/or executive group.

10 There needs to be a follow-up one year later (maximum) on the results of the action plan. If this involved using different methods of recruitment or advertising, it would be necessary to alter the applicants' equal opportunities form to ask how they became aware of the vacancy. This is in order to assess whether the new advertising has had any effects on the visibility of the organisations' vacancies.

Voluntarism or legal requirements

Underlying this issue about monitoring is the bigger question of how the UK should enforce its societal commitment to equal opportunities in employment. Although there has been legislation, until recently, much of the UK's approach to equal opportunities in the workplace has rested on voluntary participation by employers. Arguments have been offered that providing equal opportunities has a business case. It gives employers access to the widest possible pool of talent from which to recruit. Also, in the climate where shareholders have started to be more concerned stakeholders about company policies, a further argument is that organisations' workforces need to reflect the population of shareholders, as well as their local communities. While there is acceptance of the value of such arguments on behalf of many employers, this project has shown that relatively few are prepared to put resources into effective monitoring of workplace equal opportunities. Voluntarism only takes us so far. It has taken us to the point where many, if not most, UK employers will espouse they are committed to equal opportunities. But they are not prepared to move to the point where they will put additional resources into ensuring they have the most diverse workforce possible. Clearly, to go further than their current position would add to their costs though it may also produce savings by ensuring well targeted equal opportunities policies.

The problem with facing additional costs through taking monitoring seriously is it needs additional business benefits to show it is worth it. The USA example provides the evidence that, without the push of legislation, it is hard to move things forward.

USA employers noted how things changed substantially after contract compliance legislation came into force, with the requirement for affirmative action plans and annual equal opportunities reports. USA employers reported to Hepple *et al.*'s (2000) study:

> Affirmative action became a mainstream business matter because it was linked with gaining government contracts.
>
> The affirmative action plan became a strategic business plan used internally to focus where action was needed. It produced an impetus for change.
> (Hepple *et al.*, 2000, p. 123)

Another employer's representative said that their representation of women and minorities had doubled since adopting affirmative action plans in the 1970s. The legislation effectively created a clear business case for non-discriminatory behaviour. Whether this case was already present, and prejudiced employers did not realise it, is difficult to tell in retrospect.

While it is clear that voluntarism on its own is unlikely to move us forward in offering the workforce equal opportunities in employment, there are still a number of options about where to go from here. Many UK commentators, while prepared to support equal opportunities, are not happy to advocate a USA approach. Hepple *et al.* (2000) argue for a middle way. They want to shift the responsibility onto organisations and individuals to change themselves. Thus they argue that:

> Anti-discrimination measures should be augmented by positive duties to promote equality which do not depend upon proof of fault by an individual. These positive duties should aim at securing fair participation of under-represented groups in the workforce, fair access to education, training, goods, facilities and services and a fair distribution of benefits.
> (Hepple *et al.*, 2000, p. xiv)

Overall, their aim was to offer proposals that seek to encourage an inclusive, proactive, non-adversarial approach to achieving fair participation and fair access. The framework they proposed starts from a base of persuasion, information and voluntary action plans. Where these fail, Hepple *et al.* (2000) suggested moving to equality commission investigations, compliance notices, judicial enforcement and sanctions and withdrawal of contracts or subsidies.

What they suggested for the early stages is that employers with ten or more full-time employees should be required to conduct a periodic review (once every three years) to find out whether there is significant under-representation of women, ethnic minorities or disabled people. In the USA, of course, this is an annual requirement and the terminology is 'underutilisation'. Hepple *et al.* (2000) suggested that an employment equity plan be drawn up, in consultation with interest groups such as employees and their representatives, where under-representation is found.

It is the view of these authors that this is a good way to move forward. However, in addition to the Hepple *et al.* framework, we suggest that employers need to collect the necessary data about their workforce and applicants. Achieving this could be done, as in the USA, by legislating to force employers to collect data. Alternatively, all employers could have a duty to monitor, which would necessitate such data collection. This is a baseline necessity if the Hepple *et al.* (2000) framework is to have a chance of being effective. In addition, since it is vital that data are complete, employers may need to be given the legal rights to require prospective employees to provide the necessary data about themselves. If employers already collected applicants' and employee data, it would not be such a large step to analyse it.

Notes

Chapter 1

1 The research found considerable variation by size of organisation and sector: job title/grade analysis by ethnic group (total 22 per cent; small and medium-sized enterprises [SME] 18 per cent; large 35 per cent; industrial 25 per cent; services 20 per cent); job title/grade analysis by gender (total 31 per cent; SME 26 per cent; large 47 per cent; industrial 31 per cent; services 31 per cent).

2 Hoque and Noon (2001) used the 1998 Workplace and Employment Relations Survey conducted by the Department of Trade and Industry.

Chapter 2

1 It might be possible to check the accuracy of this assumption using Health Survey data.

2 One EO manager is quoted as saying: 'Preparing affirmative action plans was a defining moment'.

Chapter 3

1 In June 2005, a new survey, the Annual Population Survey (APS), was published. This is based on the LLFS incorporating a further boost sample. It may offer better opportunities for analyses than have previously been possible.

2 We have been advised that Government Register Office Scotland (GROS) did not have a delay of this length.

Chapter 4

1 It is possible that some of the applications are from the same individuals.

References

Berthoud, R. (2000) 'Ethnic employment penalties in Britain', *Journal of Ethnic and Migration Studies*, Vol. 26, No. 3

Bhavnani, R. (1994) *Black Women in the Labour Market. A Research Review*. Manchester: Equal Opportunities Commission

Brown, C. and Gay, P. (1985) *Racial Discrimination: 17 Years after the Act*. London: PSI

Burchardt, T. (2000) *Enduring Economic Exclusion: Disabled People, Income and Work*. York: York Publishing Services/Joseph Rowntree Foundation

Burchardt, T. (2004) *Being and Becoming: Social Exclusion and the Onset of Disability*. London: Centre for Analysis of Social Exclusion, London School of Economics

Cabinet Office (2003) *Ethnic Minorities and the Labour Market*. London: Cabinet Office

CRE (Commission for Racial Equality) (2001a) *The Duty to Promote Race Equality: A Guide for Public Authorities*. London: Commission for Racial Equality

CRE (2001b) *Code of Practice on the Duty to Promote Race Equality*. London: Commission for Racial Equality

CRE (2002a) *Ethnic monitoring – A Guide for Public Authorities*. London: Commission for Racial Equality

CRE (2002b) *Public Procurement and Race Equality*. London: Commission for Racial Equality

CRE (2003a) *Public Authorities and Partnerships: A Guide to the Duty to Promote Race Equality*. London: Commission for Racial Equality

CRE (2003b) *Formal Investigation Reports – Employment*. London: Commission for Racial Equality

CRE (2003c) *Towards Racial Equality*. London: Commission for Racial Equality

Coombes, M. (1997) 'Monitoring equal employment opportunity', in V. Karn (ed.) *Ethnicity and the 1991 Census: Employment, Education and Housing among Ethnic Minorities, Vol. 4.* London: HMSO

Coussey, M. and Jackson, H. (1991) *Making Equal Opportunities Work.* London: Pitman

Dex, S. (1992) *The Costs of Discriminating against Migrant Workers: An International Review.* World Employment Programme Working Paper. Geneva: International Labour Organisation

DfEE (Department for Education and Employment) (2001) *Age Diversity.* London: DfEE

DLA (2003) *Workforce Equality and Diversity.* London: DLA

DRC (Disability Rights Commission) (2004) *Disability Briefing.* Manchester: DRC

DWP (Department for Work and Pensions) (2002) *Older People Statistical Information.* London: DWP

DWP (2003a) *The Geography of Ethnicity.* London: DWP

DWP (2003b) *Ethnic Minorities in the Public Sector.* London: DWP

EFA (Employers Forum on Age) (1999) *Employer Awareness of the Code of Practice on Age Diversity.* London: Employers Forum on Age

Employment Policy Foundation (1991) *Basic EEO Resource Manual: Practical Guidance for EEO Professionals and Attorneys.* Washington DC: Employment Policy Foundation

EOC (Equal Opportunities Commission) (2000) *25 Legal Cases.* Manchester: EOC

Esmail, A. and Everington, S. (1993) 'Racial discrimination against doctors from ethnic minorities', *British Medical Journal,* Vol. 306

Esmail, A. and Everington, S. (1997) 'Asian doctors are still being discriminated against', *British Medical Journal,* Vol. 314

Goodlad, G. and Riddell, S. (2005) 'Social justice and disabled people: principles and challenges', *Social Policy and Society,* Vol. 4, No. 1, pp. 45–54

Graham, P., Jordan, D. and Lamb, B. (1990) *An Equal Chance or No Chance*. London: The Spastics Society

Heath, A. and Cheung, S.Y. (2004) *Ethnic Penalties in the Labour Market, Interim Analysis*. London: Department of Work and Pensions

Hepple, B., Coussey, M. and Choudhury, T. (2000) *Equality: A New Framework, Report of the Independent Review of the Enforcement of UK Anti-discrimination Legislation*. Cambridge: University of Cambridge, Centre for Public Law and the Judge Institute of Management

Hirst, M., Thornton, T., Dearey, M. and Maynard Campbell, S. (2004) *The Employment of Disabled People in the Public Sector: A Review of the Literature*. York: Social Policy Research Unit, University of York

Home Office (2003) *Race and Equality, The Home Secretary's Employment Targets*. London: Home Office

Hoque, K. and Noon, M. (1999) 'Racial discrimination in speculative applications: new optimism six years on', *Human Resource Management*, Vol. 9, No. 3

Hoque, K. and Noon, M. (2001) 'Ethnic minorities and equal treatment: the impact of gender, equal opportunities policies and trade unions', *National Institute Economic Review*, April

Hurstfield, J., Meager, N., Aston, J., Davies, J., Mann, K., Mitchell, H., O'Regan, S. and Sinclair, A. (2004) *Monitoring the Disability Discrimination Act*. Brighton: Institute for Employment Studies

Jewson, N. and Mason, D. (1995) *Formal Equal Opportunities Policies and Employment Best Practice*. DfEE Research series, No. 69. London: DfEE

JNCHES (Joint Negotiating Committee for Higher Education Staff) (2004) *Race Equality Communication and Consultation Report for Higher Education Institutions*. Joint Negotiating Committee for Higher Education Staff and Equality Challenge Unit report. London: Universities and Colleges Employees' Association (UCEA)

Jones, T. (1993) *Britain's Ethnic Minorities*. London: Policy Studies Institute

Joseph, E. (2003) *What's on the Agenda? How UK Directors Contribute to Social and Environmental Objectives*. London: Institute for Public Policy Research

Liff, S. (1999) 'Diversity and equal opportunities: room for a constructive compromise', *Human Resource Management Journal*, Vol. 9, No 1

Modood, T. and Berthoud, R. (1997) *Ethnic Minorities in Britain, The Fourth National Survey of Ethnic Minorities*. London: Policy Studies Institute

Noon, M. (1993) 'Racial discrimination in speculative application: evidence from the UK's top 100 firms', *Human Resource Management Journal*, Vol. 3, No. 4

Owen, D. (1994a) *Ethnic Minority Women and the Labour Market: Analysis of the 1991 Census*. Manchester: Equal Opportunities Commission

Owen, D. (1994b) *National Ethnic Minority Data Archive, 1991 Census Statistical Papers*. Warwick: University of Warwick, Centre for Research on Ethnic Relations

PIU (Performance and Innovation Unit) (2000) *Winning the Generation Game*. London: Performance and Innovation Unit, Cabinet Office

Simpson, L. and Dorling, D. (1994) 'Those missing millions: implications for social statistics of non-response to the 1991 Census', *Social Policy*, Vol. 23, pp. 543–67

Smith, A. and Twomey, B. (2002) 'Labour market experience of people with disabilities', *Labour Market Trends*, Vol. 110, No. 8

Stevenson, W.G., Mallon, J.R. and Hepper, F. (1988) 'Practical aspects of monitoring equality of employment opportunity in a large organisation', *The Statistician*, Vol. 37, No. 3

TUC (Trades Union Congress) (2003) *Law Change Could Help Get One Million Disabled People into Work*. London: TUC

Appendix 1: Employer interviews – topic guide

Background: pre-interview preparation

Nature of business, size, main sites, workforce, recruitment practices, equal opportunities policies.

Screening over telephone

What data are collected about applicants for your different jobs?

We are looking for at least some employers who collect/record and store data about applicants for jobs, which includes: minority group, gender.

Main topics to cover

1 Background: confirm nature of business and types of jobs covered in business. Number of sites. If possible get a profile of workforce; numbers in different jobs (ask in advance). Ask about minorities, gender, age and disability in each groups? Is it known? Can you see the numbers? *If public sector*, get insight into how they are interpreting their new duties under the Race Relations Amendment Act to collect data and monitor position of ethnic minority groups (either here or under EO below).

2 Talk through recruitment process from deciding need to employ/replace staff member to getting someone in post. Do by a number of jobs of different levels. Any outsourcing? (Check later about how this affects EO policies/data collected about applicants.)

3 Focus on *criteria used* in recruiting staff to (range of) different jobs. Are these set out in writing anywhere? How far do they correspond with educational levels/ qualifications? Role of experience? Age?

4 Focus on *spatial areas* for recruitment of (range of different) jobs. Where do expect job *x* employees to live? Do they ever investigate where employees live, travel distances, etc. Advertising used and its spatial coverage? Specific names required for follow-up later to check their spatial coverage.

5 Databases/records kept about applicants and staff – type of staff and level. Records about applicants? (All jobs?) By minority, etc. status? Stored? How long? Possible to link to who gets the job? Does it follow people through the company? Does it update their circumstances (e.g. marital status)? How easy to pick out distributions of current staff by grade/job; minority status; gender; age; disability status?

6 Equal opportunities policies and practices: collect any written documents about EO policies/statements. How are these monitored? Training for managers? Recruiters? Regular or one-off? Records? Examined? What done? Whose job? Whose responsibility? Targets (even if informal) ever used?

7 Barriers they saw to using the Census data and even to collecting data from applicants.
- Has the employer done anything to see what the barriers are (e.g. investigating working practices, culture)?
- Union representatives may have a different view about the barriers.
- Employers' views on what would need to be done to do more than window dressing (or form filling) about equal opportunities?
- Need to find the drivers/champions in each organisation who could take a strategic view on how to get things done.
- What sort of output from the Census would help them in analysing equal opportunities?

Appendix 2: Questions and codes of key variables in datasets

The variables of interest in the 2001 Census and Labour Force Survey (2001 onwards) are defined as shown in Table A2.1.

Table A2.1 Variables of interest in the 2001 Census and Labour Force Survey (2001 onwards)

2001 Census	2003 LFS
Ethnicity	
White	Same as 2001 Census
British	
Irish	
Other white	
Mixed	
White and black Caribbean	
White and black African	
White and Asian	
Other mixed	
Asian or Asian British	
Indian	
Pakistani	
Bangladeshi	
Other Asian	
Black or black British	
Caribbean	
African	
Other black	
Chinese or other ethnic group	
Chinese	
Other ethnic group	
Disability	
1 Limiting long-term illness or disability	1 DDA disabled and work-limiting disabled
2 Economic activity (last week)	DDA disabled
Permanently sick or disabled	Work-limiting disabled only
	Not disabled
	2 Current disability only
	Current and past disabled
	Past disability only
	Not DDA disabled

(Continued)

Table A2.1 Variables of interest in the 2001 Census and Labour Force Survey (2001 onwards) (continued)

2001 Census	2003 LFS
Highest qualifications	

2001 Census	2003 LFS
No qualifications	No qualifications
Level 1	1 Access level
Level 2	2 Intermediate level 1
Level 3	3 Intermediate level 2
Level 4/5	4 Higher
Other qualifications/level unknown	5 Advanced higher

* The highest level of qualification variable uses both the educational and vocational qualification question, and the professional qualifications question

Includes a range of detailed questions on type of qualifications and can be recoded to Census categories

No qualifications: no academic, vocational or professional qualifications

Level 1: 1+ O levels/CSE/GCSE (any grade), NVQ level 1, Foundation GNVQ

Level 2: 5+ O levels, 5+ CSEs (grade 1), 5+ GCSEs (grade A*–C), school certificate, 1+ A levels/AS levels, NVQ level 2, intermediate GNVQ

Level 3: 2+ A levels, 4+ AS levels, high school certificate, NVQ level 3, advanced GNVQ

Level 4/5: first degree, higher degree, NVQ

Levels 4–5: HND, HNC, qualified teacher status, qualified medical doctor, qualified dentist, qualified nurse, midwife, health visitor

Other qualifications/level unknown: other qualifications (e.g. City and Guilds, RSA/OCR, BTEC/Edexcel), other professional qualifications

Professional qualification (England and Wales)

0 Does not have professional qualification

1 Has professional qualification

Scottish qualifications are coded differently

Geography

2001 Census	2003 LFS
LA for limited variables on SAR and lower for tabular output. GOR otherwise	LA for limited variables (Local Labour Force Survey) and region otherwise
North East	Tyne & Wear
North West	Rest of Northern region
Yorkshire and the Humber	South Yorkshire
East Midlands	West Yorkshire
West Midlands	Rest of Yorkshire and Humberside
East	East Midlands

(Continued)

Table A2.1 Variables of interest in the 2001 Census and Labour Force Survey (2001 onwards) (continued)

2001 Census	2003 LFS
South East	East Anglia
South West	Inner London
Inner London	Outer London
Outer London	Rest of South East
Wales	South West
Scotland	West Midlands (metropolitan county)
Northern Ireland	Rest of West Midlands
	Greater Manchester
	Merseyside
	Rest of North West
	Wales
	Strathclyde
	Rest of Scotland
	Northern Ireland

Occupation (all compatible – SOC)

SOC sub-major (2) (public use SAR)	SOC major groups (1)
Corporate managers	Managers and senior officials
Managers and proprietors in agriculture and services	Professional occupations
Science and technology professionals	Associate professional and technical
Health professionals	Administrative and secretarial
Teaching and research professionals	Skilled trades occupations
Business and public service professionals	Personal service occupations
Science and technology associate professionals	Sales and customer service occupations
Health and social welfare associate professionals	Process, plant and machine operatives
Protective service occupations	Elementary occupations
Culture, media and sports occupations	
Business and public service associate professionals	Unit SOC (4)
Administrative occupations	Senior officials in national government
Secretarial and related occupations	Directors and chief executives of major organisations
Skilled agricultural trades	Senior officials in local government
Skilled metal and electronic trades	Senior officials special interest organisations
Skilled construction and building trades	Production, works and maintenance managers
Textiles, printing and other skilled trades	Managers in construction
Caring personal service occupations	Managers in mining and energy
Leisure and other personal service occupations	Financial managers and chartered secretaries
Sales occupations	Marketing and sales managers
Customer service occupations	Purchasing managers
Process, plant and machine operatives	Advertising and public relations managers
Transport and mobile machine drivers and operatives	Personnel, training and industrial relations managers
Elementary trades, plant and storage related occupations	Information and communication technology managers
Elementary administration and service occupations	Research and development managers
	Quality assurance managers
	Customer care managers
	Financial institution managers
	Office managers

(Continued)

Table A2.1 Variables of interest in the 2001 Census and Labour Force Survey (2001 onwards) (continued)

2001 Census	2003 LFS
SOC minor (3) (in-house SAR)	Transport and distribution managers
	Storage and warehouse managers
Corporate managers and senior officials	Retail and wholesale managers
Production managers	Officers in armed forces
Functional managers	Police officers (inspectors and above)
Quality and customer care managers	Senior officers fire, ambulance, prison, etc.
Financial institution and office managers	Security managers
Managers in distribution; storage and retailing	Hospital and health service managers
Protective service officers	Pharmacy managers
Health and social services managers	Healthcare practice managers
Managers in farming; horticulture; forestry and fishing	Social services managers
	Residential and day care managers
Managers and proprietors in hospitality and leisure services	Farm managers
	Natural environment and conservation managers
Managers and proprietors in other service industries	Managers animal husbandry, forestry, fishing, n.e.c. (not elsewhere classified)
Science professionals	Hotel and accommodation managers
Engineering professionals	Conference and exhibition managers
Information and communication technology professionals	Restaurant and catering managers
	Publicans and managers licensed premises
Health professionals	Leisure and sports managers
Teaching professionals	Travel agency managers
Research professionals	Property, housing and land managers
Legal professionals	Garage managers and proprietors
Business and statistical professionals	Hairdressing and beauty salon managers and proprietors
Architects; town planners; surveyors	
Public service professionals	Shopkeepers, wholesale and retail dealers
Librarians and related professionals	Recycling and refuse disposal managers
Science and engineering technicians	Managers and proprietors in other servcs, n.e.c.
Draughtspersons and building inspector	Chemists
IT service delivery occupations	Bioscientists and biochemists
Health associate professionals	Physicists, geologists and meteorologists
Therapists	Civil engineers
Social welfare associate professionals	Mechanical engineers
Protective service occupations	Electrical engineers
Artistic and literary occupations	Electronics engineers
Design associate professionals	Chemical engineers
Media associate professionals	Design and development engineers
Sports and fitness occupations	Production and process engineers
Transport associate professionals	Planning and quality control engineers
Legal associate professionals	Engineering professionals n.e.c.
Business and finance associate professionals	IT strategy and planning professionals
Sales and related associate professionals	Software professionals
Conservation associate professionals	Medical practitioners
Public service and other associate professionals	Psychologists
Administrative occupations: government and related organisations	Pharmacists and pharmacologists
	Ophthalmic opticians
Administrative occupations: finance	Dental practitioners
Administrative occupations: records	Veterinarians
Administrative occupations: communications	Higher education teaching professionals
Administrative occupations: general	

(Continued)

Table A2.1 Variables of interest in the 2001 Census and Labour Force Survey (2001 onwards) (continued)

2001 Census	2003 LFS
Secretarial and related occupations	Further education teaching professionals
Agricultural trades	Education officers, school inspectors
Metal forming; welding and related trades	Secondary education teaching professionals
Metal machining; fitting and instrument making trades	Primary and nursing education teaching professionals
Vehicle trades	Special needs education teaching professionals
Electrical trades	Registrars and senior admin. educational establishments
Construction trades	
Building trades	Teaching professionals n.e.c.
Textiles and garments trades	Scientific researchers
Printing trades	Social science researchers
Food preparation trades	Researchers n.e.c.
Skilled trades n.e.c. (not elsewhere classified)	Solicitors and lawyers, judges and coroners
Healthcare and related personal services	Legal professionals n.e.c.
Childcare and related personal services	Chartered and certified accountants
Animal care services	Management accountants
Leisure and travel service occupations	Management consultants, actuaries, economists and statisticians
Hairdressers and related occupations	
Housekeeping occupations	Architects
Personal services occupations n.e.c.	Town planners
Sales assistants and retail cashiers	Quantity surveyors
Sales-related occupations	Chartered surveyors (not quantity surveyors)
Customer service occupations	Public service administrative professionals
Process operatives	Social workers
Plant and machine operatives	Probation officers
Assemblers and routine operatives	Clergy
Construction operatives	Librarians
Transport drivers and operatives	Archivists and curators
Mobile machine drivers and operatives	Laboratory technicians
Elementary agricultural occupations	Electrical and electronic technicians
Elementary construction occupations	Engineering technicians
Elementary process plant occupations	Building and civil engineering technicians
Elementary goods storage occupations	Quality assurance technicians
Elementary administration occupations	Science and engineering technicians n.e.c.
Elementary personal services occupations	Architectural technologists and town planning technicians
Elementary cleaning occupations	
Elementary security occupations	Draughtspersons
Elementary sales occupations	Building inspectors
	IT operations technicians
	IT user support technicians
	Nurses
	Midwives
	Paramedics
	Medical radiographers
	Chiropodists
	Dispensing opticians
	Pharmaceutical dispensers
	Medical and dental technicians
	Physiotherapists
	Occupational therapists

(Continued)

Table A2.1 Variables of interest in the 2001 Census and Labour Force Survey (2001 onwards) (continued)

2001 Census	2003 LFS
	Speech and language therapists
	Therapists n.e.c.
	Youth and community workers
	Housing and welfare officers
	NCOs and other ranks
	Police officers (sergeant and below)
	Fire service officers (leading officer and below)
	Prison service officers (below principal officer)
	Protective services associated professionals n.e.c.
	Artists
	Authors, writers
	Actors, entertainers
	Dancers and choreographers
	Musicians
	Arts officers, producers and directors
	Graphic designers
	Product, clothing and related designers
	Journalists, newspaper and periodical editors
	Broadcasting associate professionals
	Public relations officers
	Photographic and audio-visual equipment operators
	Sports players
	Sports coaches, instructors and officials
	Fitness instructors
	Sports and fitness occupations n.e.c.
	Air traffic controllers
	Aircraft pilots and flight engineers
	Ship and hovercraft officers
	Train drivers
	Legal associate professionals
	Estimators, valuers and assessors
	Brokers
	Insurance underwriters
	Finance and investment analysts and advisers
	Taxation experts
	Importers, exporters
	Financial and accounting techicians
	Business and related associate professionals n.e.c.
	Buyers and purchasing officers
	Sales representatives
	Marketing associate professionals
	Estate agents, auctioneers
	Conservation and environmental protection officers
	Countryside and park rangers
	Public service associate professionals
	Personnel and industrial relations officers

(Continued)

Table A2.1 Variables of interest in the 2001 Census and Labour Force Survey (2001 onwards) (continued)

2001 Census	2003 LFS
	Vocational and industrial trainers and instructors
	Careers advice and vocational guidance specialists
	Inspectors factories, utilities and trading standards
	Statutory examiners
	Occupational hygienists and health and safety officials
	Environmental health officers
	Civil Service executive officers
	Civil Service administration officers and assistants
	Local government clerical officers and assistants
	Officers non-government organisations
	Credit controllers
	Accounts and wages clerks, bookkeepers
	Counter clerks
	Filng and other records assistants and clerks
	Pensions and insurance clerks
	Stock control clerks
	Transport and distribution clerks
	Library assistants and clerks
	Database assistants and clerks
	Market research interviewers
	Telephonists
	Communication operators
	General office assistants or clerks
	Medical secretaries
	Legal secretaries
	School secretaries
	Company secretaries
	Personal assistants and other secretaries
	Receptionists
	Typists
	Farmers
	Horticultural trades
	Gardeners and grounds(wo)men
	Agricult and fishing trades n.e.c.
	Smiths and forge workers
	Moulders, core makers, die casters
	Sheet metal workers
	Metal plate workers, shipwrights, riveters
	Welding trades
	Pipe fitters
	Metal machine setter and setter-operator
	Tool manufacturers, tool fitters and markers-out
	Metal working production and maintenance fitter
	Precision instrument makers and repairers
	Motor mechanics, auto engineers
	Vehicle body builders and repairers

(Continued)

Table A2.1 Variables of interest in the 2001 Census and Labour Force Survey (2001 onwards) (continued)

2001 Census	2003 LFS
	Construction operatives n.e.c.
	Heavy goods vehicle drivers
	Van drivers
	Bus and coach drivers
	Taxi, cab drivers and chauffeurs
	Driving instructors
	Rail transport operatives
	Seafarer (merchant navy), bridge, light, boat
	Air transport operatives
	Transport operatives n.e.c.
	Crane drivers
	Fork-lift truck drivers
	Agricultural machinery drivers
	Mobile machine drivers and operatives
	Farm workers
	Forestry workers
	Fishing and agriculture related occupations n.e.c.
	Labourers building and woodworking trades
	Labourers other construction trades n.e.c.
	Labourers in foundries
	Industrial cleaning process occupations
	Printing machine minders and assistants
	Packers, bottlers, canners, fillers
	Laboratories, process and plant opertions n.e.c.
	Stevedores, dockers and slingers
	Other goods handling and storage occupations n.e.c.
	Post worker, mail sorting, messenger, courier
	Elementary office occupations n.e.c.
	Hospital porters
	Hotel porters
	Kitchen and catering assistants
	Waiters, waitresses
	Bar staff
	Leisure and theme park attendants
	Elementary personal services occupations n.e.c.
	Window cleaners
	Road sweepers
	Cleaners, domestics
	Launderers, dry cleaners, pressers
	Refuse and salvage occupations
	Elementary cleaning occupations n.e.c.
	Security guards and related occupations
	Traffic wardens
	School crossing patrol attendants
	School midday assistants
	Car park attendants
	Elementary security occupations n.e.c.
	Shelf fillers
	Elementary sales occupations n.e.c.

Appendix 3: Supplementary tables associated with figures in Chapter 4

Table A3.1 Energise technical staff recruitment figures 2003–04, and 2001 and SAR 2001 Census data for given populations

	Energise 'technical' category 2003–04	2001 SAR Census, EWN, NVQ 4/5, 20–59	2001 SAR Census, EWN, NVQ 4/5+ technical*, 20–59	2001 SAR Census, EWN, technical*, 20–59	2001 SAR Census, NW, technical*, 20–59
Applicants					
Men	77.9	50.1	82.1	81.6	83.2
Women	22.1	49.9	17.9	18.4	16.8
Total %	100	100	100	100	100
N	12,121	205,665	10,177	22,924	2,939
Hires					
Men	73.6				
Women	26.4				
Total %	100				
N	197				
% applicant men hired	1.5 (*n* = 9,437)				
% applicant women hired	1.9 (*n* = 2,684)				

Source: SAR 2001 individual SAR 3 per cent sample England, Wales or NI. Qualification levels differ in Scotland and are provided separately in the SAR data and not included here. Age 20–59.
EWN: England, Wales or Northern Ireland
NW: North West region only.
NVQ 4/5: highest qualification levels NVQ levels 4 or 5.
* Technical occupations defined from SAR as SOC minor codes 212, 211 and 311.